Portrait of a Jewish Scholar

SOLOMON L. SKOSS

1884 1953

Portrait of a Jewish Scholar

Essays and Addresses

by

SOLOMON L. SKOSS

NEW YORK
BLOCH PUBLISHING COMPANY
5717 — 1957

Library of Congress Catalogue Card Number: 57–9819

PRINTED IN THE UNITED STATES OF AMERICA
PRESS OF Maurice Jacobs INC.
224 N. 15TH ST., PHILADELPHIA 2, PENNA.

Foreword

PROFESSOR Solomon Skoss was every inch a scholar, but his scholarship did not express his total personality. That personality had broader human facets which deserve to be recorded, exemplified and kept alive. When, therefore, Dr. Skoss asked us in his will to sift his popular essays and addresses and see them published in a form that would make them available to the general public, we undertook to do so. Mrs. Skoss, of course, gave us much help.

Most of these essays were delivered before the members of the *Dorshei Daʿat* (Seekers for Knowledge) Society of Philadelphia; we think that others as well will accept them with as much pleasure as did those who heard them from the lips of our dear and honored friend. We have added a number of his articles of an entirely different kind, for example, two of his essays on bee-keeping. We did so in order to illustrate our late friend's versatility and breadth of knowledge which we admired and which, we are sure, others will admire too.

SOLOMON GRAYZEL
SAMUEL N. KRAMER
JOSEPH REIDER

Contents

Foreword v

Solomon L. Skoss — A Biography, by *Solomon Grayzel* 3

Incidents in the Life of Doctor Skoss, by *Irene K. Skoss*. 23

Professor Skoss — A Tribute, by *Abraham I. Katsh* 36

On Jewish History and Personality

1. The Recently Discovered Hebrew Scrolls near the Dead Sea in Palestine 41
2. The Early Linguistic History of the Jews 51
3. The Karaites in Jerusalem in the 10th and 11th Centuries 66
4. A New 10th-Century Reference to the Jews Praying at the Temple Site in Jerusalem 74
5. An Ethiopic Book of Magic 77
6. Judah Halevi 80
7. Adolph Sutro, Civic Leader and Bibliophile 91
8. The Treatise of Maimonides on Health Care 99

On Islam and the Moslems

9. Mohammed's Night Journey from Mecca to Jerusalem 117
10. The Prohibition of Wine in the Mohammedan Religion 125
11. Moslem Pilgrimage to Holy Cities 133

On Bee-keeping

12. Bee-keeping in the Holy Land in the Time of Jesus . . 137
13. Swarming — A Study in Bee Behavior 141

Glossary 149

Biographical Notes

Solomon L. Skoss — A Biography

By Solomon Grayzel

1. *Foundations of Character.*

THE WORD "Siberia" has an ominous sound in the ears of those who know Russia. One thinks of dreary, snow-covered wastes, of men condemned to a living death far from home, of exiles, political and criminal, dragging themselves through a meaningless existence until the day of release from the watchful eye of a tyrannical government. Yet it seems that childhood could find a paradise even in Siberia and that the love of learning, courage and idealism enough to last a lifetime could be transmitted there as elsewhere.

It is hard to fathom what induced Samuel Skoss to go to the little town of Tshusovaya in the province of Perm, on the Siberian side of the Ural mountains. Family tradition has it that he could have succeeded to his father-in-law's rabbinic post, but that he refused it in favor of his wife's uncle. Casting about for means of earning his livelihood, he discovered how limited were the economic opportunities in the town of Horki, in the province of Mohilev, which he then called home. At about that time it became known that a liberal governor of the Siberian province of Perm had recognized the legitimacy of the religious needs of the small number of Jews who lived there; he graciously granted them permission to obtain the services of a rabbi and *shoḥet* (ritual slaughterer). That is how Samuel Skoss and his young wife, Blumeh (*née* Teitzlin), came to settle there in 1877. Before long children began to come, among them a son by the name of David and, two years later, in 1884, another son who was given the name of Zalman-Leb after a relative who had been a distinguished talmudical scholar.

It must have been clear from the outset that one could not thrive on being a religious functionary for a small community of Jews. Samuel Skoss ventured into business, for which there was ample opportunity in that underdeveloped country, and he prospered. Having solved the economic problem, he was able to solve also the more important problem of the education of his sons. When the boys were old enough, probably about the age of five, a teacher was imported for them and, no doubt, for whatever other Jewish children that lived in the vicinity. Zalman-Leb enjoyed those years of schooling; but unfortunately they were too few. Before long the teacher left — or was compelled by the government to leave. To Samuel Skoss this, of course, represented a tragedy. It was unthinkable that his sons would not study Torah. The only possible solution to the problem was for himself to undertake the teaching of his sons.

It is open to question whether a father is a desirable teacher for his children. His eagerness to transmit information is likely to exceed his patience. Unable to blame the teacher, the combined father-teacher is likely to vent his disappointment on his pupils. Only the very pliant child can profit from such an arrangement. In the Skoss case, the situation was aggravated by the father's need to absent himself on business, while the indulgent mother failed to enforce attention to the assignments which he left for the children to cover. Zalman-Leb, quiet, studious, not given to energetic games because of a tendency to quick fatigue, managed to absorb enough to earn the father's praise. David, however, the older boy, was restless and inattentive; he attended to his work at the last possible moment, and he therefore bore the brunt of his father's anger. The teaching sessions over the weekend were recalled many years later with some bitterness. Nevertheless, the father's influence had clearly been effective: the sons did learn the basic lessons of Jewish life. He did plant within them the foundations of Jewish knowledge and character.

The growing Skoss family — there were five children now — was doing quite well, when a change in the government of Russia upset everything. A change in government policy during the early 1890's resulted in a decree that none but those condemned to exile might live in Siberia and that, in any event, Jews were not to be welcomed there. The Skoss household was given three days to settle its affairs and vacate the home they had built up in the course of a decade and a half. It meant disposing practically overnight of the house and its surrounding acreage, of household goods and anything else that could not be transported easily. The non-Jewish neighbors knew when they had the advantage; they offered prices which were not only ridiculous but downright insulting. In his bitterness of heart Samuel Skoss simply set fire to everything. The children never forgot the scene of the house, where they had spent so many years, going up in flames as their wagon pulled away from it.

They returned to the mother's home town of Horki in the province of Mohilev, Zalman-Leb being then about ten years old. The great advantage of the new situation was that the boys could now continue their education in the *yeshiva* (rabbinical academy) at Dubrovna, a town near by. They made the usual progress there, though somehow, probably half stealthily, they acquired along with their knowledge of the Talmud also a reading and writing knowledge of Russian. Zalman-Leb returned home for his thirteenth birthday. But the celebration over, and his bar-mitzvah status attained, he went back to continue his talmudic studies at Dubrovna where his brother had preceded him. Here the two brothers lived through the typically Jewish experience of making physical sacrifices for the attainment of knowledge; usually the house of study served also as dormitory and its bare benches as beds. Food was provided by the town's Jews, who never questioned their obligation to feed the bodies of the hungry minds. David, still the rebel, chafed at the enforced preoccupation with the Talmud; Zalman-Leb drank it all in with an avidity which in retrospect appears both natural and providential.

After two years at the *yeshivah*, the seventeen-year-old and the fifteen-year-old returned home. But to what prospects? What did Russia offer a Jewish boy? The professions were closed, except to the very few. Trade required capital. The boys were fortunate enough to find a few private lessons, but their sole prospect was to join the large class of *Luftmenschen*, men who lived on thin air. They had plenty of time; there was nothing that had to be done in a hurry; so that they spent much of their day at the local *beth-midrash* (house of study), presumably in further study of rabbinic texts, but actually in long and fervent discussion of affairs which were then agitating the Russian-Jewish world. For that was the period of storm and stress for the Jewish youth of the czarist empire.

Two movements within Jewish life affected the young Skoss boys, each movement sufficient to disturb, if not destroy, the traditional Jewish views and ways. On the one hand, Herzlian Zionism was transforming the age-old longing for redemption into an active striving for self-emancipation. On the other hand, there was the lure of Haskalah (Enlightenment) which expressed itself in impatience with the circumscribed culture of the Jewish environment and a consuming eagerness to become part of the western world. There was a third movement also, an external one: the growing impatience with czarist rule on the part of Russia's progressive forces which had many sympathizers among the country's Jewish youth. All three movements could well combine in the mind of an intelligent young Jew, since all three were at bottom expressions of a prevalent hunger for democracy and broader culture. Among the *baḥurim* (students) at the *yeshivot* there were long discussions; the *bet midrash* became a secret club house.

There went on at the same time a frantic and basically hopeless effort to solve the problem of one's personal future. The town of Horki had acquired a new Jewish physician who placed himself at the head of the Zionist movement. Zalman-Leb, however, was more interested in the new library which this physician organized, and which contained many classics of the day in Hebrew translation. He became an avid reader and, what was more important, he there and then decided to acquire the western languages needful to embark upon the alluring sea of general culture. He began with German and French; later, when emigration to America increasingly loomed as the only solution for the personal problem, the study of English was added. All this was done privately, without the aid of a teacher and without any particular system. Zeal and perseverance made up for these lacks and partly overcame them. All that one needed was time, and the few private pupils became a source of annoyance which outweighed their usefulness as a source of income. The cooperative spirit between the two brothers was such that David, realizing how greatly his few hours of teaching interfered with Zalam-Leb's studies, undertook to relieve him of them. Presumably the sharing of the income was taken for granted. Yet the younger brother felt that somehow he must contribute to his own upkeep. His efforts to this end provided him with interesting experiences, but with little income.

Before long, David Skoss, perhaps tired of the small town atmosphere of Horki, went to Gomel and obtained a post as teacher of Hebrew and allied subjects in a modernized Jewish school. He stayed there for some months and there Zalman-Leb visited him in 1904. He arrived just in time to witness the infamous pogrom which broke out in that city and, having lived through those days of horror, the two brothers left Gomel and returned home.

David would have had to come home in any case because he had reached the age of military service. Never a pleasant prospect, it was downright dangerous for an outspoken young man like David Skoss to be inducted into the army of a government for which he had the contempt then characteristic of progressive youth, Jewish or Christian. Samuel Skoss, perhaps at David's suggestion, thereupon hit upon a plan typical of the Russian Jewish attitude of that era: the younger son would pose as the older! Since Zalman-Leb's health had never been especially good, it was assumed that the examining physicians would reject him. Thus, he would not serve, and the older brother would gain a few years to plan his emigration to America. It was a brilliant idea; but it did not work. The physicians hesitated about accepting Zalman-Leb; in the end, however, they decided that he was fit enough. And the younger, studious, rather weakly brother began an army career of close to four years, while the older and more vigorous brother was freed a year or so later, when his turn came, because according to Russian army regulations one son in a family was enough for any one time.

The army could not fail to see that Private Solomon Skoss would be more useful in the regimental office than on the parade grounds. Skoss became the official scribe for his regiment and later was promoted to the same job for the entire army group which consisted of four regiments. As such, he, of course, had both duties and privileges. One of his duties, of which he often spoke in later years, was to teach reading and writing to illiterate recruits; the peasant minds found it hard to grasp the mysteries of print and script. Moreover, the same qualities of gentleness and obedience which had endeared him to his father stood him in good stead with the commanding general. The latter found the Jewish soldier-secretary good company. He liked to talk to him, and this liking was intensified when he discovered that Skoss was an excellent chess player. This is how it came about that the general often invited the private to his quarters; and the private found it politic to let the general win an occasional game.

Russian army life of those days was fraught with dangers of a quite unmilitary kind. The revolutionary movement had penetrated the ranks, especially among the younger officers. These correctly estimated that the intelligent young Jew was bound to be sympathetic to their cause. They approached him; but he was too cagey to admit his interest until he had proved to his complete satisfaction that they were not merely laying a trap for him. Once convinced that they were in earnest, he helped them materially by copying or preparing propaganda leaflets and the like. On at least one occasion he was almost caught red-handed, but succeeded in explaining away his presence at the chancery late at night.

At long last the term of service was over. Zalman-Leb returned to his parental home and to the now unavoidable and unpostponable question of his future. Russia offered the Jew nothing but starvation and oppression; America loomed as the land of freedom and opportunity. By this time, to be sure, an intelligent Jew in Russia no longer thought of America as the land of easy success; he expected life to be hard and the struggle bitter. But at least there was a chance for life with dignity; and one trusted, if he was young enough, that opportunities would be found. David had left for the United States soon after Zalman-Leb's return home. In a comparatively short time he sent a paid-up steamship ticket for his younger brother.

2. *Years of Search.*

Zalman-Leb Skoss was twenty-four when he arrived at the port of New York in 1907. He did not stay in the immigrant-crowded city, but went to Buffalo where a boyhood friend, Sam Luskin, had established himself some years earlier. Two problems faced him: to find some means of earning a livelihood and to acquire the means for adjusting himself to the new cultural environment. In the solution of the first problem he followed the easiest course: he became a teacher of Hebrew. For the solution of the second problem the obvious first step was to master the English language. While still in Russia he had learned to read English and to understand what he read; but speaking was a more difficult art. He enrolled in a public school, not disdaining to sit in a classroom with children. His progress was rapid.

Misfortune began to dog his footsteps. He was depressed by his loneliness; he chafed under the slow, or apparently slow, progress; and, above all, the climate was not good for his frail body. One penetratingly gusty day, someone stole his overcoat and the cold which Skoss contracted proved persistent. A physician diagnosed it as pleurisy and warned him of the serious threat of tuberculosis. Skoss took the physician's advice and left for Denver, where he was soon admitted to a sanitarium. Since little was known at that time about the treatment of the dread disease, he was subjected to much experimentation and finally to an operation. He remained at the sanitarium for about a year.

To earn part of his keep while recuperating, he waited on the staff at table. But Skoss could not be without some cultural interest. The Yiddish poet Yehoash (Solomon Bloomgarden) was a fellow patient at the hospital. In and out of the sanitarium, Yehoash was carrying forward his labors on a lexicographical work which was eventually published as a dictionary of the Yiddish language, with special emphasis on its dependence upon Hebrew and Aramaic. Skoss could be and was of considerable help. Moreover, as soon as he was discharged from the sanitarium, he enrolled in the University of Denver. The practical matter of earning a livelihood was apparently of secondary importance and was not permitted to interfere with his studies. Blessed with a beautiful handwriting, he earned a meager living by painting signs and preparing display cards for shop windows. Had his ambitions lain in that direction, this might have been a first step to a successful advertising career, a business then beginning its fantastic rise. Skoss, however, was content with academic degrees; a B. A. and, a year later, an M. A. Incidentally, the M. A. got him an offer of a large salary raise from his employers, who took it literally and assumed that Skoss had graduated as Master Artist.

These goals attained, there was need for finding a permanent occupation. The need was the greater since Skoss was now a married man. While still at the sanitarium he had met a fellow patient by the name of Sarah Meyerson whom he subsequently married. He took a civil service examination and obtained the position of railroad mail clerk. Obviously this was no job for him, being beyond his strength, bad for his health and unsatisfying to his intellectual cravings. He took other civil service examinations for posts in which his linguistic abilities would be put to use; but only temporary appointments were offered him despite his high standing on the lists. He soon gave up his job with the Post-Office Department and moved to Los Angeles where the entire Skoss family had by now taken up residence.

He again drifted into teaching in a Jewish school. The income from this occupation being insufficient for his needs, he got an additional job painting automobiles. Both tasks were exhausting enough, and neither gave any promise of a career. At this point he was overwhelmed by a crushing misfortune: his wife died in childbirth, leaving him a baby girl.

A fortunate incident now brought him in touch with a man who was enthusiastic about bee-keeping. Here was a strange occupation, and Skoss was decidedly interested. He took the job offered him and entered upon a life which, on the surface, accorded not at all with his background and ambitions. What attracted him was perhaps the idea of caring for living creatures. He certainly did not regard his new occupation as merely a job; he studied the subject and became expert in it. In later years, when he was already a world-renowned authority in a completely different field, his usual smile would broaden and his chuckle would become just a bit louder when conversation happened to turn to the subject of bees.

Bees were also the subject of his first appearance in print. There was a noted apiarist by the name of Dr. Phillips who published a journal on apiculture. He happened to meet Skoss and was charmed to find in this shy man a person who really understood bee-keeping. He asked Skoss to contribute an article to his journal. The result was a dissertation on bee-keeping in the Talmud. Obviously, what surprised Dr. Phillips was not the display of talmudic erudition — he probably had no idea how extensive such knowledge had to be — but rather the fact that the ancient Jews and their rabbis had known so much about bees. This article, in turn, led Skoss to write another one, on the subject of bee ailments, which eventually, without his knowledge, found its way into a Palestinian agricultural publication. When he came to Palestine in 1925, he discovered that certain circles had already heard of him.

Unfortunately, being an apiarist, while it sometimes called for studiousness, usually required more physical strength than Skoss could command. Once, while lifting a fairly heavy hive,

Skoss let it slip out of his hands. The frightened bees stung him so hard that his entire body swelled and he was seriously ill for weeks. When he recovered, he was compelled, at least temporarily, to give up his work of which he had grown so fond. Back in Los Angeles with his baby daughter, there was nothing for him to do but go back to the teaching of Hebrew at a school conducted by the Jewish Workers' Alliance (Farband). He seemed unable to extricate himself from the net which fate had thrown about him.

3. *The New Horizon.*

What he needed, both spiritually and intellectually, was a revolutionary change, something that would save him from remaining a Hebrew teacher with unrealized dreams and thwarted ambitions. Fortunately, he found the courage to risk a plunge into the unknown. Indeed, what had he to lose?

Bee-keeping had been the one promising occupation with which he had experimented during his fifteen years of wandering and uncertainty in America, and he thought he could make a place for himself as an apiarist. He heard that a very fine course in the subject was being given at the University of Pennsylvania. He crossed the continent to enroll in that course. Undoubtedly, he was helped in making up his mind by the fact that a sister of his deceased wife, Mrs. Lewis Broudo, resided in Philadelphia and promised to look after the baby.

It was December 1922 when he arrived in Philadelphia and without wasting time went to the University to inquire about the course in entomology in which he was interested. Told that he would have to wait for the professor's return, Skoss naturally drifted into the Library and picked up a Hebrew volume. Someone tapped him on the shoulder and introduced himself as Edward Chiera, a professor in the Semitics Department.

"That's a rather unusual book," the professor remarked to Skoss. "You must be well advanced in Hebrew if you can read it." Rather amused, Skoss admitted that he had been a student of Hebrew from childhood. A conversation developed in which Professor Chiera urged Skoss to undertake the study of Arabic, while Skoss defensively urged his need to prepare himself for earning a livelihood through the study of entomology. Even while they were talking, the professor of entomology returned and made it clear that there was no intention to offer his course that semester. To Skoss this was a terrible blow; he had uprooted himself and come this long way only to find his plans shattered by a simple fact. Professor Chiera firmly and sympathetically continued to dwell on the advisability of undertaking the study of Arabic, and he was seconded by Professor James A. Montgomery who now appeared and joined the group. Skoss still insisted that he could not afford the luxury of becoming a student in a field to which he was a comparative stranger and which gave no promise of practical results. Thereupon both professors thought of the same solution to the problem: The reluctant student could enroll at Dropsie College, where tuition was free and study at which entitled one to free tuition at the University.

What could he lose, Skoss must have asked himself. As far as bee-keeping was concerned the half year would be lost in any case, while the study of languages, especially those connected with Hebrew, was still close to his heart. He was tempted. Taking the streetcar, he went to Dropsie College. Diffidently he inquired of the librarian's assistant (Miss Anna Meilachowitz) whether he could enroll as a student of Arabic. Dropsie, too was looking for promising students; at the time, in fact, the fellowship in Arabic was vacant. Miss Meilachowitz lost no time in calling Professors Chiera and Montgomery on the telephone, received their recommendation of the man they had met only that morning and Miss Meilachowitz gave him an application to fill out which, she assured him, had every chance of being accepted. A few weeks later, Skoss, still amazed at the turn of events, appeared before Dr. Adler. The latter, always practical even though as eager as anyone to encourage study, was the first to point out difficulties. After all, Skoss was already in his thirty-eighth year and he was undertaking the study of a difficult language with which he was completely unfamiliar. But Skoss' earnestness was persuasive and reassuring; he never struck anyone as irresponsible. He emerged from the interview the holder of a fellowship in Arabic at Dropsie College and a student of Arabic grammar at the University of Pennsylvania. It was a far cry from his hopes of becoming an apiarist; his life was completely transformed.

He rented a room near the home of his sister-in-law, so that he could see his little Teddie (Theodora) daily. The ten dollars a week which the Dropsie fellowship brought — five hundred dollars a year — obviously did not suffice. He looked for a position teaching Hebrew in an afternoon school conducted either by the Jewish community or by a synagogue. Such positions were to be had, and Skoss was never without one; but it cannot be said that he enjoyed teaching in such schools. He could not come to terms with the inadequate teaching content and with the lackadaisical teaching methods. But all such problems and difficulties were secondary now that he had a goal. The study of Arabic took hold of him; it absorbed and obsessed him.

The professor of Arabic at Dropsie College was then Benzion Halper, a person of great charm and vast learning, deeply interested in his few and devoted pupils. Under him Skoss specialized in Judeo-Arabic, that mixture of Hebrew and Arabic which had been the common speech of the Jews who lived in touch with the Moslem civilization during the Geonic and subsequent periods. It was a perfect linguistic combination for a person with Skoss' background, as it was with Halper's, so that the two hit it off famously. Tragically, however, Dr. Halper died in 1924, and Skoss was left without any direct guidance in his own research. His subsequent achievements and, especially, the broad scholarship he displayed in his doctoral thesis, are therefore all the more remarkable.

It was only natural that he should now want to perfect himself in the language and literature to the study of which he had decided to dedicate himself. Dropsie College was able to provide him with a fellowship for study abroad and he soon (1924) left for Cairo. He plunged into study, attending whatever classes he could at the University, but for the most part working in libraries, both public and private. A brief visit to Palestine rounded out a highly profitable tour. This great intellectual experience was brought to a fitting conclusion with the receipt of a cable from Dr. Adler inviting Skoss to join the faculty of the College as the successor to the lamented Benzion Halper. His thesis was accepted by the Dropsie College faculty and he was granted his doctorate in 1926, when he assumed his duties.

4. *Scholar and Teacher*.

Skoss assumed his duties at Dropsie College in a spirit of whole-souled dedication. The number of his pupils was small and most of them were mature and deeply interested in the subject. What they needed was guidance and stimulation rather than outright classroom instruction. Skoss was perfectly suited to this type of teaching. He was involved in their problems of research and they became concerned with his. It was, on the whole, a perfect situation for a graduate department.

The field of Judeo-Arabic had hardly been touched in many centuries; even during the past century of renaissance in Jewish scholarship the number of men who had cultivated this field could be counted on the fingers of one hand. Men and books that had played a crucial role in the development of Bible exegesis and Hebrew grammar during the early Middle Ages had become mere names, so that a vast and interesting aspect of the life of the Jews was veiled in darkness. Of special interest were the Karaites, those heretics in Judaism who rejected rabbinic law and limited themselves to the Written or Scriptural Law. Thus compelled by their religious attitude to make careful study of the Hebrew language and to penetrate the meaning of the Bible text, the Karaites served as a goad to the Rabbanites. Karaite writings of the early Middle Ages were therefore of surpassing cultural and religious importance. Skoss was soon recognized as the foremost authority in this field; both his outstanding works were contributions to it.

His first book, *The Arabic Commentary of Ali ben Suleiman the Karaite on the Book of Genesis*, his doctoral dissertation, practically re-discovered an influential scholar about whom modern scholars did not know even the century during which he flourished. Skoss offered information, not only on the author himself, but also on his language and manner of thought. Indeed, the book described and shed light on an exegetical movement, on the one hand, and existing facilities for studying it, on the other. A curious by-product of this work, and an example of Skoss' scholarly acumen, was his success in piecing the old book together out of two manuscripts, the one part in New York and the other in Leningrad.

Ali ben Suleiman's commentary was but an introduction to an infinitely greater and more basic work, the *Agron*, or dictionary, of David ben Abraham of Fez, to which Skoss devoted in effect all the rest of his life. David ben Abraham was a Karaite who, though born in Fez, Morocco, lived in Palestine towards the end of the eleventh century. This dictionary, like so many other works of the early medieval scholars who wrote in Arabic, had been lost for centuries, until it was re-discovered about a hundred years ago in two copies among old collections of discarded manuscripts in Jerusalem. Skoss' edition of it, with his introduction and notes, makes it an invaluable source for knowledge of the development of Hebrew during the early Middle Ages, of the language spoken among the Jews and of Bible exegesis. Like the commentary of Ali ben Suleiman, this was a pioneer work.

One can view the handsome two volumes, produced with the help of the Kohut Foundation by the Yale Oriental Series, and have no idea of the intense and protracted labor which was required to prepare them. The American Council of Learned Societies defrayed the cost of photographing the codices and of visiting Leningrad whose library had to be used if the work was to be done properly. Several visits to the libraries of Oxford and Cambridge were also necessary for the purpose. Once the material was collected, in the form of photostats and copies tediously made by hand, it had to be deciphered, compared, every word studied, noted and arranged. The difficulty of the work is evident from the very simple fact that it took so diligent a scholar as Skoss from 1928 to 1945 to bring these two volumes to completion. At that, the work was not quite completed, for Skoss still hoped to produce a third volume containing a glossary and index.

But another project intervened. One cannot work in the field of Judeo-Arabic literature without becoming increasingly aware of the vast influence exercised on medieval Jewish thought and literature by Saadia Gaon. When therefore Skoss, in the course of his researches, came across manuscript material of hitherto incompletely known works by this great Gaon, he made up his mind to make this material available. One can understand that the temptation to do so was irrepressible. Skoss turned to Saadia's work in Hebrew grammar, in which field, as in so many others, the Gaon had been a pioneer. Again our meticulous scholar worked steadily for a number of years. Several chapters of the work were published in the *Proceedings of the American Academy for Jewish Research.* Due to the devoted efforts of Mrs. Irene Skoss, these chapters were produced in book form posthumously.

There was so much he still planned to do, so many manuscripts he still hoped to edit, so much hidden knowledge he still wanted to reveal. Perhaps other scholars will complete the work for which he laid the foundations. In any case, those who will labor in the field of Judeo-Arabic in the future will always remember him with gratitude. Ultimately, a scholar can expect no more.

5. *The Man and his Personality*

No one who knew Skoss had the slightest doubt that he enjoyed the twenty-seven years of teaching and scholarly activity. In a very real sense these years compensated for the struggle and insecurity and disappointment which had been his lot until this opportunity came. His personality expanded as recognition came. He loved to talk about his work, especially to those who could appreciate the complexity of the scholarly problems which he had to solve. Not only his own work, his classes at Dropsie College also served as a source of gratification. This modest man seemed to be proud of being able to open the gates of an area of knowledge to men and women who knocked at the door.

His personal life, too, now ran more evenly. Upon his return from his student journey to Cairo and as he assumed his duties at the College, he married Miss Irene Kapnek who proved an extraordinarily understanding and devoted companion to him and an excellent mother to his child. They established an unpretentious household at 1135 W. Wyoming Avenue, in the Logan section of Philadelphia. The very choice of the house offers an indication of Skoss' romantic attachment to his scholarship. There were other houses he might have chosen; but this house happened to be identified with a number which marked the year of Maimonides's birth, and this proved to be the deciding factor.

Jealous though he was of his time, he and Mrs. Skoss loved to entertain, especially his students at Dropsie College, and the visitor always found there an intelligent and varied company. Conversation rarely lagged and, if it ever did, Skoss had at his command a fund of anecdotes about his experiences in various countries and libraries or about his early life and struggles. He was never bitter.

Hardships, to be sure, were not altogether at an end. The great depression which began in 1929 entailed the loss of his meager savings. Skoss, however, had learned the value — or, rather, the lack of value — of money as long as health and happiness remained untouched. Much more difficult to bear was the poverty of Dropsie College, the profound service of which the American Jewish community never quite appreciated and, therefore, never properly supported. Throughout those difficult years of the depression, the faculty of the College was dreadfully underpaid. It was hard to keep smiling; it was even harder to keep house. But Mrs. Skoss managed, while Skoss now found useful the habits of parsimony which he had acquired years before. He begrudged himself a ride where he could walk and counted a luxury what others considered a necessity. It should be recorded, however, that the Skosses never refused a request for charity. Nor did he hesitate, then or later, to invest in a book or to photostat a manuscript bearing on his subject or within his field of interest. These he classed with the necessities, although he must have suspected that he would never have the time to work on them.

In time the economic situation improved. Dr. A. A. Neuman, Dr. Adler's successor in the presidency of Dropsie, was constrained to make public appeal to the Jewish community. The economic situation having improved, and the College having been brought more forcefully to their attention, the Jews of the United States came to the relief of this exceptional institution, still not in the measure to which it was entitled, but at least sufficiently to enable the faculty to live more comfortably.

The hardest blow was a heart ailment which struck Skoss in the early 1940's. For weeks he was confined to his bed; for months he could do little teaching and little work on his beloved manuscripts. Slowly he recovered and, although he was not prevented from undertaking several journeys to foreign libraries and to Israel, he always had to be careful.

One of Skoss' most obvious characteristics was modesty. There are those who, having attained a bit of success, become insufferable; here was a man who, by dint of personal effort, had realized the dreams of his youth and gone beyond them, becoming recognized as an authority in a very difficult field. Yet he remained mild, even shy and self-deprecating, at least about everything but his field of knowledge. To see this was a tonic and a lesson. There was also something youthful about him, and his chuckle over a funny story or a cartoon in a newspaper was contagious. He kept hundreds of clippings containing such pictures and anecdotes and would go back to them and enjoy them time and again.

The only expensive pleasure, relatively speaking, which he permitted himself was music. He went to the Philadelphia Orchestra concerts often and enjoyed them intelligently. His one other pleasure was in the company of people whose conversation was lively without being frivolous. That is why he joined and frequently attended the meetings of the *Dorshei Da'at*. This group of Philadelphians met monthly on Saturday evenings to discuss a current or historical paper prepared by one of their number. The members were for the most part Jewish professionals and a few businessmen, representing a wide variety of viewpoints and interests. It would have been contrary to Skoss' nature to try to overawe them with his scholarship; they, on the other hand, were the type that respected a man of learning. His simplicity endeared him to them. Before this group he read a number of papers on subjects related to his interests and experiences.

He passed away on the last day of Passover. Having returned from synagogue and gone up to his room to rest, he suffered a heart attack and was gone in a matter of minutes. It is a tribute to the care which his wife had given him that he survived his first attack by thirteen years. His friends could at least be grateful that he had been spared that much longer to brighten and enlighten the world. And now his memory remains for a blessing.

Incidents in the Life of Doctor Skoss as Told by His Wife

Besides attending classes at the Dropsie College and the University of Pennsylvania, Skoss taught daily at the Folk Schule. The heavy schedule began taxing his not too abundant strength, and he decided to undertake teaching children privately instead. So it happened that three of his pupils were the children of my relatives, Mr. and Mrs. Max Waber whom he taught between the hours of five and six. If he had no immediate engagement or other pupils after those lessons, he had a standing appointment to have dinner with these people. As I too was a frequent dinner guest there, that is where I had the good fortune of meeting Solomon L. Skoss.

After I got to know him, I was intrigued by his store of knowledge on many phases of life, but especially Bible, history and Hebrew learning. We were inhabitants of two different worlds — he the typical, modest yeshivah *bochur* of European environment; I, more or less, a career woman of the modern business world of America. I did not come from a rabbinical family and I had not had much formal education, but I was immediately attracted to Skoss because of his scholarship as well as his wit and charm. What he found to interest him in me I'll never understand, except that he admired my modesty and my liberal views. After paying several visits to my business establishment and observing my methods of serving humanity and the relationship between the people I employed and myself, he was rather amazed to find such characteristics in a person of my position and background. I found him deeply sympathetic and understanding. I was also impressed with his devotion to his child and his attempt to be both father and mother to her. He liked my liberality and what he frequently called my "good horse sense" — an indefinable something which one is only born with and that cannot be acquired or attained through learning or education.

As time went on and we got to know each other better, we found that we were attracted to each other. He brought his child around and I became attached to her.

About a year and a half later, unfortunately for Skoss, his teacher and guide, Professor Benzion Halper, passed away. He was left on his own to proceed with a very complicated thesis. It was very difficult, and so, before handing it in, he appealed to Professor Henry Malter for assistance. But Doctor Malter happened to be a political opponent of the man on whom Skoss based his thesis — a man who had lived in the 10th century! ! ! — and that was his excuse for refusing to assist Skoss. However, the thesis was approved and Skoss did graduate.

Skoss was not satisfied with this accomplisment. By this time he was so enraptured with the study of Arabic that he felt he had to delve further into it. He appealed to Doctor Adler for a fellowship to go to Cairo, Egypt, to continue his Arabic studies there. Fortunately, this was granted to him. A more jubilant person I had never seen. He lost no time in making his arrangements, although he found it very difficult to leave his child. With my assurances that I would keep a watchful eye on her, off to Cairo he went.

He took courses at the Egyptian University and at the American School of Oriental Studies. While there he met a wealthy banker, Mr. Jack Mosseri. This man possessed an enormous library of rare books and manuscripts. He became interested in Skoss and invited him to visit his library and even to make photostats of some of his rare manuscripts. Mr. Mosseri also referred Skoss to Salomon David Sassoon of India and England, who also had an enormous library in Semitics and rare manuscripts. He lost no time in communicating with that illustrious family from whom he succeeded in getting photostats of their rare manuscripts.

Through his correspondence with that unusual family, he was invited to visit them, whenever he came to England, at their home in Letchworth — an invitation which we finally accepted on our last trip to England. We were invited, together with about 30 or 40 other guests, to tea and were asked to remain until the other guests had departed. My husband and I and the rabbi who taught Hebrew to the children of the family were then accorded the privilege of visiting their library, which was in their private chapel in their home. Mr. Sassoon showed us many illuminated and unusual manuscripts, but the greatest treasure was an illuminated codex written by a scribe in about the 13th or 14th century. He was not only an able scribe but a great artist as well. It was illuminated in pure gold and other lovely colors. The yellows, purples, blues and reds were pure extracts of fruits and vegetables. The scribe had spent 18–20 years preparing it and it is impossible to describe it, but the beauty of it is unforgettable. It had been purchased by one of the Sassoons from an old man in Baghdad, some three or four generations ago. The sum paid was not disclosed, but by this time it is priceless. Only about a hundred people have had the pleasure of viewing this marvelous masterpiece. The volume is enormous. It took several hours to turn the pages — each one more beautiful than the preceeding — on which we feasted our eyes.

It was also through Mosseri and Sassoon that Skoss learned about the great treasures in Leningrad and other European libraries. It was then that he decided that he would one day go through the great libraries of the world, first through those in Russia and then those of the other countries.

While a student in Egypt, he was selected by the student body of the American School of Oriental Studies as its delegate to the opening of the Hebrew University in Jerusalem. What an honor and a thrill that was to Skoss who had always dreamed of going to Palestine — and here he was! When he came to Jerusalem, he met friends whom he had known in Russia and through them he learned that his article on bee-ailments had been published in Palestine. They were practising the method that he recommended; unfortunately, he found that they didn't quite understand his theory and he proceeded to enlighten them and help them in their bee-keeping.

He had many unique experiences while in Palestine. One stands out as particularly charming. Friends took him by horse and cart from one small village to another to examine the bee-hives. While on the road, they saw an Arab lying on the ground, apparently ill. Skoss suggested that they stop and give the poor man aid or a lift. The others objected to this, but to accommodate their guest they finally consented. They stopped the cart and offered the Arab a ride to the next community. After the Arab got into the cart, Skoss thought he had a good opportunity to practice his Arabic, with all its complicated conjugations and grammatical forms, on a real Arab. He kept asking the stranger questions pertaining to his health. "What is wrong with you?" he asked. "Do you have a headache?" "Do you have a stomachache?" Finally the old man looked up and said to Skoss in his colloquial Arabic, "I am an Arab, but I can't understand your speech!" The others in the cart said, "You are having quite a conversation!" Skoss then related the exchange of conversation to them and they all had a good laugh about it. Whenever he related this incident, he would chuckle like a boy.

In Cairo Skoss also learned about Professor Paul Kokowzeff and decided that one day he would go to Russia to meet him. He immediately entered into correspondence with the Professor and, through a voluminous exchange of letters, they became good friends. It was in 1932 that Skoss finally got to Leningrad and there he found a wealth of additional fragments of the dictionary of the Bible, *Kitāb Jāmi al-Alfāz* of David b. Abraham Al-Fāsi, on which he was working.

While Skoss and Professor Kokowzeff were studying these fragments in the Library of Leningrad, Skoss unearthed another fragment which he studied for a time and then handed it to Professor Kokowzeff. They peered at each other for a moment and Kokowzeff said, "Is this it?" Skoss replied, "Yes, it is!" It was a small fragment of Saadia Gaon's Hebrew Grammar — the first Hebrew grammar ever written. Kokowzeff remarked, "To think that these fragments have been here 60–70 years and hundreds of scholars have gone through them, and to think that you were the one to recognize this little scrap of parchment as the thing the world has long been wondering about!"

Skoss had the reputation among scholars of putting his hands on things that were unusual. I remember comments by other scholars who said, "When Dr. Skoss puts his hands into a box of manuscripts, he comes up with unusual fragments. These various manuscripts and fragments have been in the libraries of Europe for many years and studied by many scholars, but no one seems to have found the unusual things which Skoss did." Whether it was his fundamental knowledge of Hebrew and Aramaic or pure inspiration, the fact remains that he found many treasures of which he made photostats, not only for his own use or of subjects in which he was especially interested, but he had them made, despite great cost to himself, for future students and scholars because he considered them valuable.

Many times during the night Skoss would get out of bed and

go to his study. When I would remonstrate with him about working too hard, he would reply, "But, Irene, I'm in labor! I think I've just given birth to a word!" He was referring to filling in words and sometimes sentences in old and worm-eaten fragments of the Dictionary. Often as he lay in bed, he would be inspired with the proper word. He was well rewarded when, after years of searching through the libraries, he was successful in finding additional fragments of the Dictionary which proved that his inspiration in filling in the sentences had been correct. Needless to say, this filled him with delight and he rejoiced. One almost feels that this inspiration was Divine guidance.

I am recording incidents that are facts. Skoss in his belief was orthodox and yet quite liberal. Being learned in the Bible and by nature analytical, it was difficult for him to be fanatical. As a matter of fact, his father, who was a rabbi and *shohet*, was also a liberal and used to argue with the old orthodox fanatics. At one time he hoped that Zalman-Leb would become a rabbi, but at last realized that his son could never preach what he couldn't practice. His father was a very happy man when Solomon became interested in Arabic.

Fundamentally, Skoss was very much influenced by Maimonides' philosophy. His admiration for the Rambam was so great that he was sentimental about it. It has already been stated that we bought our home at 1135 Wyoming Avenue because 1135 is the birth date of Maimonides. Time and again he translated treatises from Arabic into English and Hebrew for friends and others who were writing books and who needed some of Maimonides' material. It was never a question of charging for these services. Following the precepts established by Maimonides, he considered it a privilege to make such a contribution to scientific research.

The thing he believed in and practiced was *zedakah* (charity) — to him this was the greatest *mitzvah* (commandment). He was helpful to anyone, even beyond the bounds of his meagre income. He subscribed to almost all the Jewish and Hebrew periodicals and contributed to most of the worthy Jewish organizations. As a teacher, he would help anyone who was hungry for knowledge. He assisted students and scholars all over the world who called upon him for help or enlightenment. One of his favorites was the following quotation: "It is in loving, not in being loved, that one finds his quest; it is in giving, not in being given, that one is blessed."

Once two monks came with supposedly rare finds of manuscripts. They were very secretive about them, but he finally convinced them that he would require more time for study before passing an opinion upon them. Since they didn't want to leave the manuscripts, he prevailed upon them to have photostats made. When they returned with the photostats, he studied them off and on for weeks and weeks; then he called on Dr. Cyrus Gordon and Dr. Samuel Noah Kramer and they, too, studied the documents. After a tremendous expenditure of time and energy, they all concluded that these documents were not genuine. Skoss never regretted the loss of time, because there just *was* a possibility that they would turn out to be a valuable find.

Skoss was also inspired by Spinoza and emulated him in self-discipline. He believed that really to understand a language, one must study the whole family of related languages. Thus he studied the Romance languages — Latin, French, Spanish and Italian; Hebrew, Aramaic, Arabic and other related Semitic languages; Russian, Polish, Slovak, etc.

He loved to have people around him and our door was always open to all his students. He wanted the relationship between them and himself to be that of friends rather than of teacher-student. Yet he jealously guarded his time. If I would have company too often or plan to accept too many invitations, he would always remind me that science is a very jealous mistress, that is, if he indulged himself by being up too late, it was difficult for him to concentrate on his research. He was regular in his habits of work and study and he often expressed the wish that the Jews had a monastery such as the Catholics so that he would be able to dedicate his life to research and learning.

Skoss never aspired to live up to the standards of other people materially.

He was equally well-disciplined in the spending of time as of money. He was the sort of person who, if he earned $25, would pretend it was only $20 and would save the other $5. He always had his little reserve for emergencies. Everything he did was planned with serious thought. Whenever he applied for a fellowship to go abroad to do research, it was always a year in advance. Should his grant not be approved, he always had his little savings account so that he would be able to make the trip anyway. Fortunately, every application for a grant was awarded because of the importance of his research. Even though his expenses were paid by the Philosophical Society and, at times, by the American Council of Learned Societies, he traveled and lived very modestly.

Skoss never failed to visit the synagogues no matter what country he was visiting. He also visited the poorer sections of the cities — including those in the United States. He was always interested in mingling with the Jews there and talking with them. He was sometimes amazed to meet some who were descendants of very illustrious names in history. He used to talk about these people whose ancestors had been famous for their scholarship and attainments in trade and finance, while these, their descendants, were simple tradesmen and artisans with little learning. He often wondered if this would be the pattern to be followed by the future descendants of the modern aristocrats.

I recall a trip to an Oriental conference held in Paris. Scholars from all over the world attended and Skoss was a delegate from Dropsie College. At the first meeting a Franciscan monk introduced himself to Skoss and said, "I hear that you are a Professor of Ethiopic." Skoss replied, "I only teach a beginners class." "Since you have enough knowledge to teach the language," said the monk, "I'll consider you a Professor of Ethiopic. I am a Professor of Ethiopic here in Paris at the monastery. I am inviting all the Professors of Ethiopic at this conference to be my guests." We spent a most unusual evening with the charming monk as host. Among the treasures which he displayed was a beautiful autographed portrait of the Pope as well as one of Haile Selassie.

During the depression in 1929, we lost all of our savings and the house in which we then lived. It was a terrible blow to me and I was quite heartsick about it. Skoss, on the other hand, took it very philosophically. When I commented that I couldn't understand his attitude knowing how he had denied himself physical comforts and even necessities of life for those savings. His reply was, "My dear, if I lost my sight, it would hinder me in my work; or if I lost you or Teddy, I would cry; but not over the loss of my house or money. Money is round and rolls sometimes in one's favor and sometimes to one's discomfort."

Skoss' life was full of incidents and co-incidences, the most unusual being that which resulted in his becoming an Arabic scholar. Time and again I heard Skoss relate the fantastic tale that led him from the path of bee-keeping down the halls of Arabic scholarship. He, himself, was continually amazed by the fact that he had arrived at the University of Pennsylvania in the morning planning to enroll for a course in entomology and by nightfall had found himself an applicant for a fellowship in Arabic at the Dropsie College. It seemed that he was destined to casually select and read the Hebrew volume in the University Library which attracted Professor Chiera's attention. He always felt humbly grateful to Professor Chiera and Professor Montgomery for their interest in him, their encouragement to go to Dropsie to investigate the possibilities there for him to begin his studies in Arabic, and for their unqualified recommendation. He was also deeply grateful to Miss Anna Meilachowitz, the assistant to the Librarian at Dropsie College, for her interest and encouragement. During his first interview with her, she asked if he had his college diploma as proof of his eligibility to enter a graduate school. As he produced it he laughed to himself because when he had graduated from Denver University he resented having to pay for the diploma since he could not afford it at that time. Here at last he actually had use for the diploma which he had hesitated to buy!

Never was there a person so deeply appreciative of the opportunity extended to him at Dropsie College by the fellowship awarded to him. His gratitude deepened when they granted him a further opportunity to continue his studies in Cairo. He spoke with great reverence of his teachers, especially of Professor Max Margolis, and of the interest and courtesy shown him by his associates at the college. He often resented the fact that people all over the world, as well as those in our local community, failed to appreciate the important and essential role which Dropsie College plays in the area of Jewish culture, scholarship and learning, and the lack of support given to this unique institution. I recall the time when I said to him, "Dear, with your ability to concentrate and your patience, if you were in applied science you might make a tremendous contribution to humanity." To which he replied, "But humanistic science, too, is a necessity and in my way, I, too, may make a small contribution which may be lasting."

Skoss was truly an ascetic person. His genuine modesty and humility were quite apparent. When reference was made to the importance of his work, he would just brush it aside. Upon the completion of his Dictionary, many people complimented him on his great contribution. He remarked, "I assure you it will not make a hole in the sky nor will they cheer with excitement in Heaven." One rabbinic expression he quoted frequently was, "Those who run after *koved* (honor) find that *koved* runs away from them, but those who earn it, *koved* finds them."

His modesty was equal to that of the old rabbis we read about in ancient works; his humility was equal to that of a great person. I recall one evening when we were guests at a lovely dinner party. I met there friends of mine (to whom one's bank balance or title was important) who were unknown to my husband. I introduced him as "Professor Skoss." On the way home he chastised me gently and asked that in the future I should present him as just plain "Mister" or "Doctor." "I am a Professor only in my classroom."

He was conscious of his own faults and, therefore, tolerant of human frailty. He had the patience of a saint and was a very sympathetic and understanding person, but he could be stern and strict with his students or others when he felt it was necessary to get the best results.

Despite the fact that he was of frail physique and so absorbed in his fundamental studies, he was, nevertheless, very industrious and practical. The scientific approach he utilized in his research he also applied in less glamorous fields. He was equally competent at home repairs whether it was the plumbing, electrical equipment or carpentry. No manual work was too hard nor too menial, though these were moments stolen from his research and studies.

Among his other attributes, Skoss enjoyed a keen sense of humor. He used to enjoy the "funnies" in both the English and Jewish newspapers. He related many anecdotes of his early days. While he was a student in the *yeshivah*, at about the age of 10, he was assigned to eat his Friday evening meals with a widow with three daughters about his own age, so that he could make *Kiddush* (blessing over wine) for her. The children loved to tease him. They noticed that he was bashful and so would serve his traditional bowl of Sabbath noodle soup without a soup spoon. Being too shy to complain, he would forego the pleasure of this delicacy. Finally, one of the children had trouble with her homework and came to him for help. Thereafter they became good friends and she took special pains to see that he always had a soup spoon.

Many of the children at the *Yeshivah* were not given meals by the townspeople, but *kopekes* (one or two pennies) instead. Skoss often told of the time the boys conducted an experiment. They reasoned that since whiskey and bread are both made from wheat, would one get drunk if he ate enough bread? They collected their *kopekes* and treated one hungry little fellow to a whole loaf of bread. He ate and he ate and when he had eaten his way through half a loaf, they inquired, "Velvel, are you drunk yet?" "No," he replied, "but I sure am feeling mighty jolly!"

Skoss told many stories of his days in the Russian army when he was tutoring the illiterate peasants with a simple picture book. One poor fellow whom he was trying to teach gazed for a long time at a picture of a dog, struggling to read the simple word beneath the picture. Finally he burst out with the word for cat instead of dog — Skoss was too gentle to embarrass the man by telling him that he was wrong.

I often thought that one lifetime would hardly be enough for a man with Skoss' ambition to accomplish all he planned to do. From childhood on he was plagued with many illnesses and then in the prime of his life suffered his first heart attack. Dr. Charles Wolferth, a great heart specialist, said it was miraculous that he survived. Dr. Wolferth definitely attributed his recovery to his tremendous will to complete the project he was engaged in at that time. Skoss was physically frail but mentally a giant. He was humble and unassuming.

In going through my papers in preparing these notes, I came upon a slip of paper upon which my husband had typed these lovely words to console me upon the death of Franklin D. Roosevelt:

> A righteous or great man when he dies, he dies only for his generation, that is, not he, but his generation suffers.
> He is like a precious pearl, which is lost: wherever it is, it is still a pearl, it is lost only to its owner.

One can truly say about him what he himself said on the death of F. D. R.

Professor Skoss — A Tribute

By Abraham I. Katsh

With the passing of Professor Solomon L. Skoss, of blessed memory, the world lost one of the greatest authorities of our times in the field of Judeo-Arabic literature. The Jewish people has lost an outstanding scholar and a devoted Jew, and we his students lost a gifted teacher, a sympathetic advisor and a warm friend.

Professor Skoss enjoyed the reward of a great teacher, for many of the disciples he trained themselves made their prominent mark in their fields. Originality and thoroughness were basic attributes of his life, and these intellectual virtues he inculcated in his students. He kindled in them a love for research, and he made of them diligent and industrious investigators. As a means of stimulating them in this direction, he took pains to induce them to join scholarly societies.

Toward his students he demonstrated his sincere friendship at a time when they needed him most — during the difficult period when they were engaged in writing their theses, and later when they prepared their dissertations for publication. His encouragement and guidance were of an inestimable value to them. But he was not only a kindly teacher; he was a modest and humble soul. He did not hesitate to visit his students in their homes to discuss their problems with them, and to offer suggestions. His generosity and modesty won the hearts of his students.

Professor Skoss was equally at home with his fellow scholars. When he attended a session of a learned society, everyone flocked to him, and he greeted his colleagues with genuine warmth and affection. In his absence, people also spoke of him with appreciation and admiration. This is not quite characteristic of scholars, among whom there frequently prevails a degree of envy — the "rivalry of scholars," which according to the rabbis tends to increase knowledge. The position of Dr. Skoss and his relation to his fellow academicians were unique in this regard.

Professor Skoss was a scholar of international fame. I recall, when he was in Israel as a fellow faculty member of our New York University Workshop in 1951, many prominent figures in academic life and government circles came to pay their respects. Among them was the late Professor Eliezer Sukenik, Doctor Samuel Kaufman, Professor Benjamin Mazar, and the present Foreign Minister, Mrs. Golda Meir. Yet he did not permit these visits to interfere in any way with his every-day task as a teacher of elementary Arabic. In our Workshop in Israel, Professor Skoss earned the love of his students and colleagues as he did everywhere else. He earnestly believed that anyone could acquire a good grounding in Arabic during a few brief weeks of the summer. To prove it, he took his students to observe a class in Arabic, consisting of Israeli children, taught by one of his former students. As he left, Professor Skoss said to the group, "You see, they can learn Arabic, why not you?"

As for me, I have lost a friend and mentor. To me he was more than a teacher. No father could take a greater interest in his son and glory in his achievement than did Professor Skoss in the thesis I wrote and in the volume I published, *Judaism in Islam*. Like so many others, I owe him a deep debt of gratitude which I know that I cannot repay.

This volume of popular essays and articles written by Professor Skoss is a fitting memorial to this great scholar. These pages reflect the true versatility of the man — the scholar, the teacher, the humanitarian and friend. Of him it may be truly said that he "loved people and brought them close to the Torah."

Essays and Addresses

The Recently Discovered Hebrew Scrolls Near the Dead Sea in Palestine

During the summer, or early autumn, 1947, an Arab goatherd was grazing his flock not far from the site of ancient Jericho, in the rock-strewn hills north-west of the Dead Sea. One day, while looking for a lost goat, he discovered there a cave, located in one of the gullies, or wadies, emptying into the Dead Sea, in the neighborhood of Ein Feshkha, south of Jericho. In the cave he found several jars, only a few whole, the rest all broken, containing parchment or leather scrolls, carefully wrapped in cloth and sealed with a mixture of pitch and wax. So far some eleven such scrolls are known, discovered in that cave.

Prof. Eleazar L. Sukenik, of the Hebrew University, thinks that this cave must have served as a kind of *genizah*, where torn and discarded sacred books were hidden away in accordance with ancient Jewish usage. But the good condition of some of the scrolls and the very careful manner in which they were stored away in sealed jars suggest that the cave was used rather to store a library of some Jewish sect, hidden there perhaps in time of crisis for safekeeping.

Attention is called to the very interesting fact that in a cave in the same region of Jericho a similar discovery of manuscripts was made in the third century C. E., during the reign of the Roman emperor Antoninus, the son of Severus, associated by some scholars with the one frequently mentioned in the Talmud as the friend of R. Judah the Prince. We possess Origen's report of this ancient discovery of Greek and Hebrew manuscripts; in fact the Greek version of the Book of Psalms, discovered in this cave, was used by Origen for the preparation of his Hexapla (a work in six columns for the establishment of the correct text of the Old Testament).

Prof. Sukenik first learned of the discovery of these scrolls at the end of November, 1947, when an Armenian merchant from Bethlehem appeared at the barbed wire barricade by the Hebrew University with a fragment of a scroll. During the next few days he negotiated with this man and with a Moslem dealer in Bethlehem for the purchase of five scrolls and a bundle of fragments. Some weeks after Dr. Sukenik was working on these scrolls one of the librarians of the Hebrew University told him that in August 1947 two of them had gone to the Syrian Orthodox Convent and they had been shown five scrolls by the Metropolitan (according to the Syrian story, it must have been in October). But they had considered them to be forged, so they did not think it worth while reporting about them to Sukenik. One of the scrolls Dr. Sukenik acquired is a hitherto unknown work describing in great detail a war between the Children of Light (בני אור) and the Children of Darkness (בני חשך). The length of this scroll is two meters and ninety centimeters and its height is about sixteen centimeters, the writing taking up nineteen columns. It is written on the hairy side of the coarse parchment, or leather, with lines above the letters as well as at the margins. "The Children of Light" are "The Sons of Levi, Judah, and Benjamin" who will wage war against "The Armies of Edom, Moab, Bene-Ammon . . . Philistines, and the Armies of the Kittim of Ashur." "The Kittim of Ashur" refer, according to Sukenik and Ginsberg, to the Seleucid Greeks of Syria, thus inferring that this document was composed prior to the extinction of the Seleucid kingdom in 63 B. C. It contains no title of the work nor the name of its author.

Three more short scrolls comprise one literary work, a collection of thanksgiving hymns (הודיות), likewise hitherto unknown. Each scroll contains four columns, twelve in all; they are much higher than the above mentioned scroll, measuring about 32½ centimeters in height. The hymns are very similar to several Psalms, written in classical Hebrew and plene in orthography. A peculiar spelling is כיא, with an Alef at the end. The remaining two scrolls, acquired by Sukenik, are in poor condition and they are being slowly unrolled and studied carefully.

Five other scrolls were bought by Mar Athanasius Yeshue Samuel, Metropolitan of the St. Mark's Syrian Orthodox Convent in the Old City of Jerusalem. In January, 1948, they were offered to Dr. Sukenik for sale, and he took them for a few days for examination, but due to warlike conditions in Jerusalem at that time he could not complete the negotiations. In February, 1948, they were shown to Doctors Trever and Brownlee, Fellows of the American School of Oriental Research in Jerusalem, who, together with Prof. Millar Burrows, Director of the School at that time, photographed them and made a study of their contents.

The largest and, no doubt, the most important among them is the one containing almost the complete text of the Book of Isaiah, the scroll being 23¾ feet long and consisting of 54 columns. The next largest scroll is a hitherto unknown work in Hebrew, designated by the above-mentioned scholars as "Sectarian Document." It consists of five sheets of parchment (יריעות), varying in length, originally sewn together to produce the completed scroll which measures 6 feet 1¼ inches in length by 9½ inches in height, but since it was torn into two unequal pieces, when found in the cave, it was taken as two separate scrolls. The fourth scroll is a Commentary, or Midrash, on the Book of Habakkuk, and is the most beautifully preserved writing of all the scrolls. It measures about 62 inches in length by 5½ inches at its highest point, comprising 13 columns on two parchment sheets. The fifth scroll is in a very bad state of preservation, comprising a matted mass of leather fragments, hard and brittle. They were later carefully separated and were identified as three sections from the Book of Daniel, which appear to belong to two different scrolls. In addition, several fragments from some other piece of Hebrew religious literature were identified. So far no samples from this scroll have been published.

The first preliminary report about this momentous discovery was published by Prof. Sukenik with regard to the scrolls acquired by the Hebrew University under the title מגילות גנוזות מתוך גניזה קדומה שנמצאה במדבר יהודה, סקירה ראשונה, ירושלים; Doctors Trever and Brownlee and Prof. Millar Burrows published their reports about the scrolls acquired by the Syrian Metropolitan, as well as studies of the texts, especially of the Book of Isaiah and of the Habakkuk Commentary, in the *Biblical Archeologist*, September 1948, and in the *Bulletin of the American Schools of Oriental Research*, October 1948, followed up in subsequent numbers.

Approximate Date of the Scrolls

When Prof. Ernest Wright, of the McCormick Theological Seminary in Chicago, showed me, in July, 1948, in Paris, some photographs of the Habakkuk scroll, I was quite impressed by its beautiful calligraphy and its legibility. Having come a few days previously from Cambridge, England, where I had a good opportunity of studying several hundred fragments of various early manuscripts in Hebrew characters, I gained the impression that the style of writing in the Habakkuk scroll should not be older than the third or fourth centuries C. E. But even then it would be by several hundred years older than the oldest manuscript of the Hebrew Bible we possess, viz. the Leningrad Codex which was written in 916 C. E.

However, scholars like Professors Sukenik, Albright, Burrows, H. L. Ginsberg, and Solomon Birnbaum, of London University, think that the Isaiah scroll, unquestionably the oldest among the discovered manuscripts, dates back to the second century B. C. E., while the Habakkuk scroll and the other manuscripts of hitherto unknown Hebrew works date within about 50 years B. C. E., or at the latest in the first century C. E. There is no question that the text of the Isaiah and Habakkuk scrolls is pre-Masoretic, but the Masora was definitely established at the end of the ninth and the beginning of the tenth centuries by Ben Naphtali and Ben Asher of Tiberias. While the text of these two scrolls agrees on the whole with our Masoretic text, it deviates from the latter in its orthography and has also some interesting additions and omissions, but nothing comparable with those found in the Septuagint of some of the books of the Old Testament. Speaking of the text of the Isaiah scroll, Prof. Burrows who made a very careful study of it, states that "it agrees with the Masoretic text to a remarkable degree in wording. Herein lies its chief importance, supporting the fidelity of the Masoretic tradition" (*BASOR*, October 1948, 16 f.). He published a long list of variant readings in the Isaiah manuscript in *BASOR*, October 1948 and February 1949, and a grammatical study of it in the last number of the *Journal of Biblical Literature* (LXVIII, 195 ff.). It seems that the scribe occasionally took liberties with the text, e. g. words repeated in the MT are sometimes not repeated in this manuscript, as 6:2 שש כנפים; 6:3 קדוש (repeated once); 8:9 התאזרו וחתו; 38:11 יָהּ; 57:19 שלום; 62:10 עברו. Burrows thinks that "such omissions may have been made deliberately by a scribe who did not have the modern scholar's concern for meter." An interesting addition is בשת after כי תחת יפי in 3:24; for מי מדד בשעלו מים in 40:12 the manuscript has מי מדד בשעלו מי ים, and it has אף אשים במדבר דרך בישימון נתיבות in 43:19 for בישימון נהרות, to mention only a few variants.

Characteristic in this text, as well as in the other scrolls of the same collection, is the addition of an Alef at the end of words. So כיא, ליא, מיא, ביא, פיא, נפשי, חרבי, עמי, אניא, ידעתיא, are often written with an Alef at the end, but not invariably so; compare נקיא Joel 4:19, Jonah 1:14, and הַקליא 1 Sam. 17:17 in MT. An Alef is likewise added to pronominal suffixes of fem. sing., as אליהא, עליהא, בניהא, אוהביהא, תנחומיהא, exactly as in Arabic, but I doubt that it is a result of Arabic influence, as Prof. Burrows is inclined to think. But the main characteristic of the texts of these scrolls is their plene orthography, reminding one very much of the orthography of the Mishnah and Midrashim.

But the early dating of these scrolls is vigorously disputed by a number of scholars, as Professors Zeitlin, my friend and colleague at Dropsie College; Orlinsky; Tur-Sinai (Torczyner), of the Hebrew University; and Lacheman. They maintain that the Isaiah scroll which is the oldest is probably not earlier than the third century C. E., and the other scrolls are even later than that, giving various reasons based on paleography and on interpretation of the texts for their opinion. Of primary importance in dating these manuscripts is the Nash papyrus of Cambridge University, a small piece of papyrus measuring 5 by 2 7/8 inches, which was first published in 1902. It contains the Ten Commandments followed by the *Shema*, the text being incomplete, and it is considered the oldest fragment of the Hebrew Bible hitherto extant. But there is a wide divergence of opinions on its dating, from Albright who dates it in the second century B. C. E. to Gerald Margoliouth who dates it in the sixth century C. E. Sukenik is inclined to date it not earlier than the first century C. E., in view of the fact that its orthography with respect to מלא (*plene*) and חסר (*defective*) is much nearer to our Masoretic text than that of the scrolls, which appear to be older. However, one should take into consideration that the form of the letters in the Nash papyrus is somewhat cursive in character, while the texts of the scrolls were carefully written by trained copyists, the letters being uncial in character, and one should, therefore, be very cautious in comparing these two types of writing to each other.

Further Developments in This Remarkable Discovery

Last February the cave where the Hebrew scrolls were found by bedouin was excavated by Mr. Lancaster Harding, Chief Curator of Antiquities of the Jordan Kingdom, and Father de Vaux, of the École Biblique in Jerusalem, presumably under the auspices of the Palestine Museum. Quantities of pottery were discovered, all belonging to two types of vessels, jars and bowls, the bowls evidently having been used as covers for the jars. Originally, there must have been in the cave some forty jars, if not more, between sixty and sixty-five centimeters high and some twenty-five centimeters wide.

"Digging was done by hand and with small instruments, mostly knives. Generally there was room for only two men to be working simultaneously. The operation was complicated by previous clandestine excavators, who last November (1948) dug up the surface of the cave to a depth of several inches in the vain hope that the bedouin had missed some scrolls. So in the debris were cigarette stubs, a little modern cloth, and scraps of newspaper which had been used to wrap food. . .

"No complete new scrolls were found, but there was part of one scroll, (which has not been unrolled) and there were hundreds of bits of manuscripts as well as a large quantity of sherds. Undoubtedly the cave was the correct one; for some of the manuscript fragments clearly belong to the scrolls which are known. Apparently the bedouin broke open all the jars and removed the manuscripts, ignoring the pieces which broke off and fell on the floor. These pieces were mixed with debris in the unauthorized excavation.

"Old material brought out was in three categories. There was a good deal of cloth, splendidly spun and woven, some of it with rolling and whipping. A few ladies who saw the cloth declared it was modern; but that it was the cloth in which the manuscripts were wrapped is clear from the fact that some of the manuscript bits were stuck to the cloth. The second category is the pottery. It is uniformly late Hellenistic, except for parts of a Roman lamp and a Roman cooking pot which evidently were left by a casual visitor who took refuge in the cave or by someone who was interested in the deposit. Possibly the Roman removed some of the manuscripts; for some of the breaks in the jars were old. The pottery consisted almost entirely of broken jars and bowls; it would seem that the bowls were used as covers for the jars. . .

"The third category is the manuscript fragments, all of them in pre-Christian script." (*BASOR*, April 1949, pp. 7–8).

Of these fragments Father de Vaux has identified bits of Genesis, Leviticus, Deuteronomy, and Judges, and he thought that he had found also a fragment of the original Hebrew Jubilees. The jars are of sufficient size, according to Mr. Harding, so that some five or six rolls could have been put into each. Consequently, the library hidden in the cave must have once been a comparatively large one, perhaps of about two hundred scrolls, of which only a very small part has been recovered. Since we know that Origen obtained Bible manuscripts from a cave "near Jericho" (in 217 C. E.), and in view of the fact that two intrusive Roman lamps and a Roman cooking pot of the second or third century C. E. were found in the present cave, Mr. Harding is willing to give some credence to the unprovable but not improbable theory that it was Origen who was responsible for removing the bulk of the library from this cave.

All the fragments identified by Father de Vaux are written in the Hebrew square alphabet, the same as the previously discovered scrolls, but with one notable exception, the fragments of Leviticus. These fragments, containing a portion of the Holiness Code, are written in the old Canaanite script, a good deal like the alphabet of the Siloam inscription. It is noteworthy that in the Habakkuk commentary the tetragrammaton and the word *El* are likewise written in this old script. Father de Vaux is, therefore, inclined to think that the Leviticus fragments belong to a much older period, perhaps to the sixth century B. C. E., if not earlier. But this view is disputed by Prof. Sukenik, who maintains that this only proves that the old Canaanite alphabet was still in use among the Jews in the second or third centuries B. C. E. concurrently with the square alphabet. He thinks that it also throws a new light upon the reason why the inscriptions on the Maccabean coins are in the old Canaanite script: it only shows that both alphabets were used concurrently during that period. Prof. Albright who examined these fragments in the British Museum last summer states: "I was much surprised at the relative length and good preservation of the fragments of the Holiness Code in Leviticus, in an archaic (or, in my opinion, archaizing) script." (*BASOR*, October 1949).

In a letter to the *New York Times* dated March 8th, 1949, Sukenik stated that four months previously he had bought for the Hebrew University the two unbroken jars of those in which the scrolls were found, one 66 centimeters, the other 48 centimeters high. Recent reports from Jerusalem state that the unrolled scroll acquired by the Hebrew University has been opened and it turned out to be the last third portion of the

Hebrew text of Isaiah, chapters 44–66. Thus we possess a second Isaiah scroll from the cave. However, according to Sukenik, the text of this scroll agrees with our Masoretic text with regard to מלא (*plene*) and חסר (*defective*), thus differing from the larger Isaiah scroll which is *plene* in its orthography. He thinks that both orthographies were current among the Jews of the pre-Christian and early Christian periods at the same time, but used for different purposes. The Masoretic orthography which is *defective* and goes back to an earlier tradition transmitted from generation to generation was more sanctified and consecrated for use in the synagogues, whereas the *plene* orthography which is easily read was in popular use among the masses for everyday reading and study.

The latest information about the fourth scroll acquired by the Syrian Archbishop is contained in the last number of *BASOR* for October. It has been definitely identified by Dr. Trever as the Aramaic text of the lost Apocryphal Book of Lamech, mentioned once in a Greek list of Apocryphal books. The names of Lamech and of his wife Bitenosh (daughter of Enosh) are mentioned twice. We know from the Ethiopic Jubilees that the name of the wife of Lamech was Betenos. But so far only a small fragment of this scroll has been deciphered, and it will require further study for more definite information as to its contents.

The Early Linguistic History of the Jews

DURING their long history of almost four thousand years the Jews have spoken various languages in different localities. These languages have supplanted each other under the stress of political or economic circumstances. Occasionally two or even more languages were simultaneously used by the Jews even in the same locality, whether by different classes of society or for different purposes, as in every-day speech and in literature and liturgy.

According to the biblical tradition, Ur of the Chaldees, located about 150 miles southeast of Babylon, was the home of Abraham, the son of Terah. On their way to the Land of Canaan, as Palestine was called in ancient times, Terah and his family stopped at Haran, in northwestern Mesopotamia, where he died; but his son Abraham reached his destination. He was the first to be called "the Hebrew" (אברהם העברי, Gen. 14.13), and is traditionally considered the father of the Hebrew people. This migration probably took place some time between the 18th and 15th centuries B. C. E.

What language these ancient Hebrews spoke in Mesopotamia is not known; however, some indications from circumstantial evidence point to some West-Semitic dialect which was the mother of the Aramean language.[1] We find that Bethuel, Abraham's nephew and Rebecca's father, was called "the Aramean" (הארמי, Gen. 25.20), and so also his son Laban. The heap of stones that Jacob and Laban set up as witness was called by the latter in Aramaic יגר שהדותא "the heap of witness,"

[1] Albright, *From the Stone Age to Christianity*, Baltimore, 1940, p. 182.

while Jacob called it in Hebrew גלעד (Gen. 31.47–8). Jacob is referred to in Deut. 26.5 as "a wandering Aramean" (ארמי אבד). But his son Joseph, repeatedly called by the Egyptians "the Hebrew," already refers to the new land where his great-grandfather Abraham had settled as "the land of the Hebrews" (ארץ העברים, Gen. 40.15). After the Patriarchs settled in Canaan they adopted at an uncertain time a local Canaanite dialect which was not, according to Albright,[2] identical with the standard speech of sedentary Canaanites. After many years of gradual development this vernacular became known as the Hebrew language. Isaiah still refers to it as "the language of Canaan" (שפת כנען, Isa. 19.18). It was closely akin to Phoenician and almost identical with the Moabite dialect, as can be readily seen from the inscription of Mesha, King of Moab, dating about 850 B. C. E., which was discovered in 1868.

Some light on the antiquity of the language is thrown by the Tel-el-Amarna tablets comprising letters written in the 15th century B. C. E. by the petty kings of Syria and Canaan to the kings of Egypt. These were discovered in 1887–88. They mention the invading *Habiru* (or *Apiru*), taken by many distinguished scholars as referring to the Hebrews, who were gradually conquering Palestine. Especially interesting are the letters of the king of Jerusalem, who appeals repeatedly to the Egyptian king to send him aid without delay, otherwise the *Habiru* will take over all the territories of the king. While these letters were written in Babylonian, the international language of diplomatic intercourse of that period, they contain several Canaanite, or Hebrew, loan-words, which circumstance would indicate that this language had been in use in Palestine for many years before. These cuneiform sources relate that the *Habiru* came from Mesopotamia, through the Hittite territory, into Palestine,

[2] *Ibid.*

thus confirming the biblical account of Abraham coming from Ur of the Chaldees, by way of Haran, through the territory of the Hittites (compare the story of the purchase of the cave of Machpelah from the Hittites in Gen. 23) into the land of Canaan. It should be added here that the *Habiru* are mentioned also in cuneiform documents of the 19th and 18th centuries, as well as in Nuzi and Hittite documents of the 15th to 14th centuries B. C. E. Julius Lewy,[3] who made an extensive study of the *Habiru* mentioned in the Nuzi documents, is inclined to connect them with the Israelites of the Exodus from Egypt. Perhaps the rabbinic tradition mentioned in Midrash Rabbah on Exodus (Sec. XX, 10) that some of the tribe of Ephraim made an earlier attempt to enter Palestine, but were destroyed by the Philistines at Gath (compare I Chron. 7.21), has its hazy origin in the reports about the sporadic invasions of Palestine by the *Habiru*, or early Hebrews.

Still more significant for the early history of the Hebrew language are the Ras Shamra inscriptions on clay tablets which were discovered by French archeologists at ancient Ugarit, on the north coast of Syria, between 1929 and 1939. These tablets, dated about the 15th to 14th centuries B. C. E., were found near the excavated remains of a temple dedicated to the god Baal. They were written in a hitherto unknown alphabet consisting of simple cuneiform characters, which have no relation whatever to the syllabic and ideographic signs of Sumerian-Akkadian cuneiform writing. The only similarity with the latter writing is that the characters are likewise made of combinations of impressions by a wedge-shaped stylus on clay tablets and they also run from left to right. It required a good deal of ingenuity on the part of two scholars, Dhorme and Bauer, to decipher these inscriptions shortly after their discovery.

[3] "Habiru and the Hebrews," *H.U.C.A.*, XIV (1939), pp. 618 ff.

They were found to be written in two languages, one a Hurrian dialect and the other a very archaic Canaanite dialect, closely related to pre-Mosaic Hebrew. Nearly all the inscriptions are of a religious character, and most of them belong to three mythological epics, which treat of the events connected with the death and resurrection of the god Baal, with the marriage of the demigod Keret, and with another demigod Daniel (Dan'el). Many scholars have contributed to the elucidation of the new material, among them Dussaud, H. L. Ginsberg, Montgomery and Harris, Goetze, Albright, and Cyrus Gordon who wrote a valuable Ugaritic grammar.

In view of the fact that the Israelites comprised an amalgamation of several tribes, some dialectal differences had gradually developed in their common language. These differences appear to have been especially pronounced in the speech of the Ephraimites, as mentioned in Judg. 12.6, where it is stated that they could not pronounce the sound *shin* and for *Shibbolet* they said *Sibbolet*, even as the Lithuanian Jews of our days have difficulty in pronouncing this sound. Perhaps the interchange of letters frequently occurring in the Old Testament in words like יצחק and ישחק (Jer. 32.26; Amos 7.9, 16; Ps. 105.9); עלז, עלץ, and עלס; שריון and סריון (found only twice in Jer. 46.4 and 51.3); ברושים and ברותים, and similar interchanges have their origin primarily in dialectal differences in the speech of the various tribes.

That writing was not an art known only to the priestly cast of the ancient Hebrews, but that the youth of the masses were also evidently instructed in it, is shown by an incident related in the Book of Judges, 8.14. In describing the campaign of Gideon against Midian, it is stated that "He caught a boy (נער) of the men of Succoth [a city in Palestine east of the Jordan, in the territory of Gad], and inquired from him; "and he [the boy] wrote down for him the princes of Succoth, and the elders thereof, seventy and seven men." We must bear in mind that Gideon lived about 1100 B. C. E., or more than 3000 years ago. Even if the Book of Judges in its present form belongs to the 7th century B. C. E., as Albright maintains, he considers the Gideon and Abimelech narratives of high historical value. Also Isaiah in his most striking prophecy on Assyria which he compares to a forest consumed by fire, states: "And the remnant of the trees of his forest shall be few, that a boy may write them down" (ונער יכתבם, Isa. 10.19). This was written in the beginning of the 8th century B. C. E.

In the course of many centuries the ancient Hebrews had forgotten the Aramaic dialect which must have been their vernacular at the time of their first invasion of Canaan. This is shown by the fact that in the year 701 B. C. E., when Sennacherib's emissary Rab-Shakeh came to Hezekiah, King of Judah, and delivered his master's message to Hezekiah's representatives, he spoke in Hebrew. But these representatives asked him: "Speak, we pray thee, unto thy servants in the Aramean language, for we understand it; and speak not to us in the Jews' language, in the ears of the people that are on the wall" (ואל תדבר אלינו יהודית באזני העם אשר על החומה, II Kings 18.26; Isa. 36.11). We learn from this that, while the higher government officials in Judea, and perhaps also the aristocracy, spoke in addition to Hebrew also Aramaic — which was the international language of that period — the common people spoke only Hebrew. In Judea, this dialect developed special characteristics in the course of time, which distinguished it from other Canaanite dialects, and it is therefore referred to as יהודית "language of the Jews."

It is more likely, however, that the primary meaning of יהודית in II Kings and in Isaiah is "Judean," referring to the Hebrew dialect of Jerusalem and presumably of Judea, which is generally called now "Biblical Hebrew" and which is praised in the Talmud.[4] It is termed יהודית, "Judean," as opposed to the dialect of the northern kingdom of Israel, which developed some linguistic peculiarities akin to the Moabite dialect.[5] At a later period, especially in such post-exilic literature as, for example, Nehemiah and Esther, the meaning of the term יהודי, יהודים, was extended to apply to Jews in general. The two instances of *Yehudim* mentioned in II Kings (16.6, 25.25) refer specifically to Judeans, and its occurrence in the latter part of Jeremiah is likewise with reference to the inhabitants of Judea.

Of the more important Hebrew inscriptions of this period, the first millennium B. C. E., the calendar inscription discovered in 1908 at Gezer, an ancient town in central Palestine, should be mentioned. Dated about 900 B. C. E., it is considered the most ancient Hebrew inscription. It contains a list of months for farming, for example, "the month of ingathering [Tishri] (ירחו אסף, [cp. חיתו ארץ, Gen. 1.24]), the month of sowing, the month of late sowing, the month of cutting flax," etc. It is written in large, bold, archaic ancient Hebrew, or Canaanite, characters, with very few of the curves found in the writing of a later period. Next in antiquity comes the inscription of Mesha, King of Moab, dated about 850 B. C. E. and discovered by the German missionary Klein at the ancient city of Dibon, in Moab. While it is written in the Moabite dialect, according to Albright, it "was scarcely more remote from the dialect of the Northern Kingdom than the latter was from the dialect of Judah, which we call 'Biblical Hebrew.' "[6] Next in chronological order come the ostraca or potsherds of Samaria, which

[4] Cf. 'Erubin 53a בני יהודה שהקפידו על לשונם נתקימה תורתם בידם, בני גליל שלא הקפידו על לשונם וגו'.

[5] Cp. Albright, *Archaeology and the Religion of Israel*, p. 41, and n. 27.

[6] *Ibid.* See also *From the Stone Age to Christianity*, p. 243.

are dated in the 9th to the 17th year of the reign of Jeroboam II, about 774–766 B. C. E. They comprise labels attached to shipments of wine and oil from different localities in western Manasseh to the palace of the Israelite King. Of greater interest than the above-mentioned inscriptions is the Siloam Inscription, discovered in 1880 in the tunnel leading into the Pool of Siloam in Jerusalem. It describes in idiomatic biblical Hebrew the digging of the tunnel and how the workers on both sides met each other. It is generally assigned to the time of Hezekiah in the beginning of the 8th century B. C. E. We find in II Kings 20.20, that Hezekiah "made the pool, and the conduit, and brought water into the city," and in II Chron. 32.30 we read "This same Hezekiah also stopped the upper spring of the waters of Gihon, and brought them straight down on the west side of the city of David." These statements evidently refer to the tunnel described in the Siloam inscription.

Of still greater significance is the remarkable discovery, in February 1935, of inscribed potsherds at Tell ad-Duweir, the site of ancient Lachish, by the late Mr. J. L. Starkey, Director of the Wellcome Archeological Expedition. These ostraca, known now as the Lachish letters, comprise original messages, or perhaps reports, written by an officer named Hosha'yahu, who was stationed in a post northeast of Lachish and Azekah, during the siege of the Chaldean army of Nebuchadnezzar, in late November or early December 589, as Albright[7] definitely dates them. They were addressed to his commanding officer Yaosh, Governor of the Lachish stronghold, who apparently controlled the defenses of the western frontiers of the Judean kingdom. The words of the prophet Jeremiah (34.7) come to mind: "the King of Babylon's army fought against Jerusalem, and against all the cities of Judah that were left, against Lachish

[7] *BASOR*, 61 (February 1936), 15.

and against Azekah; for these alone remained of the cities of Judah as fortified cities." The script of these letters is a highly developed cursive form of the Hebrew-Phoenician alphabet. This shows a long tradition of writing, perhaps going back for several centuries. The language is pure biblical Hebrew, the Judean dialect of that period, the same as that of the Siloam inscription and the pre-exilic prophets. The orthography of the Lachish letters is more archaic than that of the accepted text of the Masoretic Bible, approaching the orthography of the earlier Mesha and Siloam inscriptions, in that it employs vowel-letters more sparingly. We must bear in mind that the Masora rigidly normalized and more or less standardized the orthography of the biblical text many centuries after Hebrew ceased to be a spoken language.

It has been mentioned that in the days of Hezekiah, at the end of the eighth century B. C. E., the higher public officials and probably also the nobility spoke Aramaic. However, we find in the Book of Daniel (1.4) that, when Nebuchadnezzar took the young Judean princes and nobles into captivity in the first deportation in 597 B. C. E., he ordered his chief officer Ashpenaz to teach them the Chaldean language, by which was meant Aramaic, as shown by Daniel 2.4: "Then spoke the Chaldeans to the king in Aramaic." Meanwhile the Jews taken into Babylonian captivity had gradually settled in their new surroundings, following the reassuring advice of the prophet Jeremiah in his stirring letter to them (29.4–7): "Thus saith the Lord of hosts, the God of Israel, unto all the captivity, whom I have caused to be carried away from Jerusalem unto Babylon: Build ye houses, and dwell in them, and plant gardens, and eat the fruit of them; take ye wives, and beget sons and daughters . . . and multiply ye there, and be not diminished. And seek the peace of the city whither I have caused you to be carried away captive, and pray unto the Lord for it; for in the peace thereof shall ye have peace."

As the Jews organized their life in Babylonia in closely knit communities, they continued to use Hebrew in their daily intercourse, according to several authorities.[8] This is shown by the beautiful exilic and post-exilic Psalms (such as Ps. 22, 51, 66–70, 19.7–14, 25, 33, 34, 37; Maccabees: 44, 74–79), written in pure, flowing biblical Hebrew, as are also the great prophecies of comfort and restoration of the second Isaiah (40–66), as well as the later minor prophets. These prophecies must have been addressed to the common people who were in need of comfort and guidance, and they certainly understood the words of their spiritual leaders and teachers very well and found solace in them. It is a striking fact that no similar prophecies in Aramaic have been preserved, for the Aramaic portions of Daniel and Ezra do not contain anything remotely resembling the very eloquent and passionate addresses of the exilic prophets.

It was in Palestine, under the influence of the new settlers, whom the Assyrian king brought there after the destruction of the Northern Kingdom in 722 B. C. E., that the western Aramaic dialect had slowly penetrated among the small Jewish communities remaining there. Many of the Palestinian Jews intermarried with these settlers, as well as with the neighboring tribes of Ammon, Moab, Ashdod, and others. Thus Nehemiah (13.24) complained that the children of such mixed marriages "spoke half in the speech of Ashdod, and could not speak Hebrew (יהודית), but according to the language of each people." This would imply that normally the Jews in Palestine still spoke Hebrew in about 430 B. C. E., when Nehemiah arrived there. Intermarriage was a frequent occurrence in Jerusalem for

[8] Weiss, *Dor Dor we-Doreshaw*, I, 56; Driver, *Introd. to the Literature of the Old Testament*, p. 503, and references cited there.

several years, for in 458 B. C. E. Ezra was reproaching the Jews in that city, "Ye have broken faith, and married foreign women, to increase the guilt of Israel" (Ezra 10.10). It may be added here that the Aramaic of Daniel and Ezra is a Western Aramaic dialect of the type spoken in and near Palestine.

For some time Aramaic and Hebrew were used concurrently, but gradually the former supplanted Hebrew as the spoken language both in Palestine and among the remaining Jews in Babylonia. Yet in some isolated villages in Palestine Hebrew was still spoken as late as the second century C. E., as will be mentioned later. But apart from Palestine and Babylonia, Aramaic had penetrated also into the Jewish settlements in Egypt. Several such settlements are mentioned by Jeremiah (44.1). The Jewish colony of Elephantine (an island on the Nile) was established about 586 B. C. E., as shown by the Russian Egyptologist Struve.[9] It was an outpost on the southern boundary of Egypt, serving as a military garrison to ward off attacks from Ethiopia. The papyri discovered there in 1906–8, and published by Sachau in 1911, were all written in pure Aramaic, without any Hebraisms in it. They comprise legal documents, letters and lists of names, dated from 494 to 400 B. C. E. The letters were addressed to Bagohi who succeeded Nehemiah as Governor of Judea, to Johanan, High Priest of Jerusalem, and to the rulers of Samaria.

These papyri, dating from the period of Ezra and Nehemiah, were written in an ancient or primitive form of the Hebrew square characters. This circumstance confirms the talmudic tradition in Sanhedrin 21b: "Originally the Torah was given to Israel in the Hebrew script and in the sacred tongue; it was given again to them in the days of Ezra in the Assyrian script (בכתב אשורי) and in the Aramaic tongue. Israel chose for them-

[9] Cited by Albright in *Aracheology and the Religion of Israel*, p. 168.

selves the Assyrian script and the sacred tongue, and left to the plain people (להדיוטות) the Hebrew script and the Aramaic tongue."[10] The Talmud explains that by "the plain people" (הדיוטות) are meant the Samaritans, and by "Hebrew script" (כתב עברי) is meant כתב ליבונאה, which is taken by some authorities as referring to the Samaritan script, a modification of the ancient Hebrew or Canaanite alphabet. The change from this script to the Aramaic alphabet was not accomplished, of course, during the short period of Ezra's activity. It took a much longer time of gradual development, and for quite a while both scripts must have been used concurrently. In fact, the ancient Hebrew script continued to be used in Palestine for some centuries after the introduction of the square characters, as shown by the circumstance that it was employed on coins from the Maccabean period in 141 B. C. E. down to the Bar Kochba revolt in 132–135 C. E.

The books of Daniel and Ezra were written in a natural flowing Aramaic dialect, though with some Hebraisms interspersed here and there. But the Hebrew portions of these books show a decided decline in style and diction. Driver[11] calls attention to the fact that the great turning point in Hebrew style falls in the age of Nehemiah. A marked change in style begins to show itself in the memoirs of Ezra and Nehemiah and in the prophecy of Malachi. The change is increasingly more pronounced in Chronicles, which must have been written about 300 B. C. E., in Esther and in Ecclesiastes, though not in the same degree, the last named book containing the most striking idioms of the Mishnah. . . . This change is marked both in vocabulary and in syntax. Many Aramaic and occasionally some Persian words appear and old words assume new meanings

[10] See also Yer. Meg. 71b: אשורי יש לו כתב ואין לו לשון, עברי יש לו לשון ואין לו כתב בחרו להם כתב אשורי ולשון עברי.

[11] *Introduction to the Literature of the Old Testament*[7], p. 505.

and applications. The participial form is used more frequently to denote the present tense, instead of the imperfect form formerly employed for this purpose. The grace and fluency of the earlier writers are gone; the style becomes more forced and inelegant. Yet one meets occasionally in these books a conscious imitation of earlier works, which had been already recognized as classical.

The period of decline in Hebrew literature during the Persian and Greek rule served as a transitional period to the tannaitic literature, the chief work of which is the Mishnah, completed in 200 C. E. The institution known as the Great Assembly, initiated by Ezra, continued its activity into the third century B. C. E. Many interpretations of old biblical laws, as well as new ordinances which are embodied in the early tannaitic literature, have their origin in this Assembly, whose watchword was: "Be deliberate in judgment, raise up many disciples, and make a fence round the Torah."[12] Hebrew having been supplanted by Aramaic in everyday use, the public reading of the Torah on Saturdays and holidays had to be accompanied by an oral translation into the vernacular of the people, which was called Targum. A tradition in the Talmud,[13] ascribed to Rab (3rd cent. C. E.), traces this custom to Ezra, interpreting the verse in Nehemiah 8.8: "And they read in the book, in the Law of God, distinctly; and they gave the sense, and caused them to understand the reading," as referring to the Targum. At any rate, its reading during public service dates from the time of the Second Temple. Hebrew is called in the Talmud לשון קדש "the holy tongue," and Aramaic — לשון חול "secular or everyday language"; occasionally it is called לשון סורסי, "Syriac language." Yet, in the course of time, Aramaic likewise assumed some degree of sanctity, though less so than Hebrew, which

[12] Aboth I, I. [13] Megillah 3a.

was associated with the Old Testament. The *Ketubah* and the *Get* (marriage contract and bill of divorce), very old legal documents — the form of the *Ketubah* dating back perhaps to the fourth century B. C. E. — are written in Aramaic. Several prayers in this language are incorporated in our prayer-book, the most important among them are יקום פורקן and the קדיש which, however, are of comparatively late origin.

The only parallel in Jewish history to the quasi-sanctification of Aramaic is Yiddish. This Judaeo-German dialect, dating back to the 14th century, if not earlier, has assumed in the course of many centuries a kind of intimacy almost bordering on sanctity with the Orthodox Jews in eastern Europe and their immigrants to the United States. The *Korban Minḥah*, a prayer-book with an old-Yiddish translation, and the numerous *Teḥines*, are used by every strictly Orthodox Yiddish-speaking woman. The *Tse'ena u-Re'enah*, the homiletic interpretation of the Five Books of Moses, and several other devotional works in Yiddish, have been used by religious Jewish women for centuries. While the menfolk who understood Hebrew looked at these works somewhat condescendingly and with a superior air, they were considered sacred enough to meet the requirements of strict Orthodoxy. It is doubtful whether the same works written in any other European language would have received similar sanction and approval.

During the period of transition in Hebrew literature, another great movement was active in the Near East, the Hellenistic movement. Its first influence appeared in Palestine in the 4th century B. C. E., after Alexander the Great passed through that country. It was a kind of blending of Greek culture with the local civilization, which gave rise to a Hellenic culture at times different from that of Greece. In Palestine it influenced first the Jewish aristocracy, who adopted Greek names and customs and spoke the Greek language. But it gradually penetrated to some degree also the Jewish masses, and even the very citadel of Judaism, as one can readily judge from the very numerous Greek expressions which found their way into the Neo-Hebrew dialect of the Mishnah, and the Greek names adopted by some of the early rabbinic authorities, as, for example, Antigonos of Soko, who flourished in the 3rd century B. C. E. The several apocryphal works in Greek written during that period testify to the prevalence of this language among the Jewish cultured classes of the time.

The Hellenistic influence was greatest, however, upon the Jews of Alexandria. Not bound by national ties which were still strong in Palestine, the Alexandrian Jews slowly became assimilated. Hebrew was almost forgotten, and there was an urgent need of a Greek translation of the Bible. This was accomplished by scholars sent from Jerusalem by the middle of the 2nd century B. C. E. The translation is known as the Septuagint, because of the tradition that it was made by seventy scholars. It was somewhat reluctantly praised even by the Palestinian teachers, who stated that the Torah could not be properly translated except in Greek.[14]

The attempt of Antiochus Epiphanes to introduce pagan worship in Palestine and the resulting Maccabean revolt are too well known to dwell upon here. While Judaism finally triumphed over Hellenism, the latter left a lasting impression on Jewish thought, an impression that even the Hebrew language has not escaped. Yet, while the knowledge of the sacred tongue was gradually narrowing down as a result of the increasing encroachment of Aramaic on one side and of Greek on the other, it evidently still continued to be used in everyday speech in some outlying places in Palestine. We find in the Talmud several interesting instances which tend to show that this was

[14] Yer. Megillah 71c: בדקו ומצאו שאין התורה יכולה להיתרגם כל צורכה אלא יוונית.

the case even long after the destruction of the Second Temple. Thus the students in the academy of R. Judah the Prince had on several occasions learned the meanings of some Hebrew words from their use by his maid-servant in her daily conversation.[15]

On one occasion the students did not know the meaning of the word סירוגין until they heard this maid reproaching them, saying: עד מתי אתם נכנסין סירוגין סירוגין (how long will you enter [the house] at intervals (and not all together)? They were apparently too shy, or perhaps too embarrassed, to ask her its meaning directly, so they waited until she happened to use it in her conversation. Another time the students did not know the meaning of חלוגלוגות (purslane) until they heard the maid-servant saying to a man who was scattering his purslane: עד מתי אתה מפזר חלוגלוגך (how long will you scatter your purslane?) On still another occasion they did not understand the meaning of the verse סַלְסְלֶהָ וּתְרוֹמְמֶךָּ, in Proverbs 4.8, until they heard the maid saying to a man who was turning his hair (with his fingers): עד מתי אתה מסלסל בשערך (how long will you curl your hair?) So the students knew that סלסלה means turning the Torah in all directions, or studying it in its various aspects. It is not stated whether this maid-servant said it in a flirtatious tone, or whether she was just talkative. Several other instances are given in the Talmud, where biblical expressions unknown to, or forgotten by, scholars were in daily use in some places in Palestine centuries after the destruction of the Second Temple. However, these were only isolated cases; generally speaking, Hebrew ceased to be a spoken language since the fourth century B. C. E., its use having been limited to liturgy and literature till its gradual revival at the end of the last century. Even in literature, Hebrew had to compete with the languages spoken by the Jews in the various countries of their dispersion.

[15] Rosh Hashanah 26b, and elsewhere.

The Karaites in Jerusalem in the Tenth and Eleventh Centuries

I HAVE chosen to give you a general idea of the settlement and activities of the Karaites in Jerusalem in the tenth and eleventh centuries, for this period witnessed their highest development in literary activity in various fields of Jewish learning and gave rise to works of enduring importance, which have exercised a great influence on the Karaites all over the world for many generations. Jerusalem was their leading spiritual center, and their most eminent authorities resided there. It is no wonder then that from Jerusalem they carried on their active missionary work in other countries.

But before describing this center of Karaite activity, a few historical remarks about the origin of this sect may not be amiss. The notion until recently prevalent that Anan was the founder of the Karaite teaching is discarded by leading modern historians. The opposition to the traditional teachings of the Talmud did not originate with him. The dissatisfaction with the rigorous interpretation of the Torah as advanced by the talmudic authorities had been latent among certain classes of Jews since the Sadducees during the later period of the Second Temple. While it is true that, after the destruction of the Temple, the Sadducees lost all their influence, yet their tendencies did not die out. They continued to exist through the centuries among some sections of the Jewish population in the Orient.

It was these survivals of the Sadducean opposition to the rigorous traditional teachings of the Talmud that Anan consolidated and organized, thus effecting an open breach with rabbinic Judaism. In fact, the small group that followed this leader in all his teachings were called "Ananites"; the name "Karaim," or Karaites, was adopted later, when Benjamin of Nahawend (830) solidified the new sect, which assumed the appellation "Bene Mikra," the Children or Followers of the Scriptures, who subsequently were referred to as "Karaim," Scripturists, as against the Traditionists, or Rabbanites ("Rabbanim"). Benjamin abandoned the unqualified opposition of Anan to rabbinic tradition and occasionally followed the latter, especially on questions of the calendar, against the teaching of Anan.

The fact that this schism took place primarily as a protest against the rigorous interpretation of the Law by the followers of the rabbinic tradition did not prevent the Karaites from interpreting the Law with greater severity than the Rabbanites. Very religious and ascetically inclined, their early leaders increased the number of fast days during the year, abstained from eating meat except that of deer and pigeons, allowed no lights to be kindled on the eve of Sabbath, thus remaining in darkness, and insisting that all food on that day be eaten cold. The forbidden degrees of relationship as a bar to marriage were also extended. Claiming to be literalists in the interpretation of the Law, they nevertheless ridiculed the Rabbanites who took the verse in Deuteronomy 6.8: "And thou shalt bind them for a sign upon thy hand, and they shall be for frontlets between thine eyes" in a literal sense, as a commandment to put on phylacteries. The Karaites insisted that this verse should be taken as a metaphorical expression, the same as the verse in Proverbs 3.3: "Let not kindness and truth forsake thee; bind them about thy neck, write them upon the table of thy heart"; both verses, according to their interpretation, signify that one should keep the respective admonitions constantly in one's mind and practice them continually.

The settlement of the Karaites in Jerusalem most likely began in the ninth century, during the time of Benjamin of Nahawend. These early Karaite settlers hailed from Babylonia and Persia, where the sect originated, and for that reason their quarter in the Holy City was known as "the quarter of the Easterners." The whole aim of the Karaite settlement there was to lead a truly religious life, as they conceived it, and to spend the days in lamenting the Exile (*Galuth*) and in praying for its restoration. They were known as *Abele Zion*, the Mourners of Zion. Eating meat was strictly prohibited in Jerusalem, since this was, in their opinion, permissible only during the time when sacrifices were being offered on the altar of the Temple. Even in the *ketuboth* of the rare marriages of Rabbanites to Karaites a clause was inserted to insure that the Rabbanite partner of the new home would keep this prohibition.

The number of the early Karaite settlers in the Holy City was, however, rather small. It was only after the arrival in Jerusalem of their eminent leader, Daniel b. Moses al-Kumisi, in the beginning of the tenth century, that their settlement grew in importance. The appeals of Daniel, as well as of his successors, brought a larger influx of Karaites into Palestine, and especially into Jerusalem, and their center grew both numerically and spiritually. The Karaites would vie with the Rabbanites in pious living and asceticism, and the environment was favorable for such a mode of life. There was also keen intellectual rivalry concerning the theological ideas of Judaism and the interpretation of the Bible, the Karaites adhering to the old precept handed down by Anan חפישו באוריתא שפיר, "Search the Scriptures diligently." This rivalry gave rise also to an extensive polemical literature.

As far as we know, Daniel b. Moses al-Kumisi was the first Karaite author of note to settle in Jerusalem. It is not known at what age he left Persia and how long he lived in the Holy

City. He was a prolific writer and had an independent attitude towards his predecessors, Anan and Benjamin of Nahawend, many of whose views he combated. Daniel al-Kumisi wrote commentaries in Hebrew on almost all the books of the Bible, of which only fragments on various books have been preserved in the Leningrad Library and among the Genizah fragments. He also composed a *Sefer ha-Mitswot* and a tract containing an appeal for a larger Karaite settlement in Jerusalem, already mentioned.

This appeal apparently met with a ready response, for a number of leading Karaite scholars settled in Jerusalem during the tenth century. First among them was the prominent Bible commentator Salmon b. Yeruhim. He wrote in Hebrew and in Arabic a very interesting polemical work, directed against Saadia Gaon and known by the title of *Sefer Milhamot ha-Shem*, "The Book of the Wars of the Lord." Its Hebrew text was edited and published some years ago by Prof. Israel Davidson, who was inclined to think that it was written in 934, while the Gaon was still alive. Several years later, in 940–50, he wrote commentaries in Arabic on some of the books of the Bible. He was very pious and extremely intolerant, so in his Arabic commentary on Lamentations I found the following passage: "Many Jews are at present desecrating the Sabbath by using lights and candles in their houses on that day, eating foods cooked on Sabbath, cohabiting with their wives, reading secular books, playing chess and other games, scaling walls and climbing trees, swimming, carrying candlesticks and candles in their dwellings, talking idly (*siḥat ḥullin*), walking around in streets and alleys, and doing other things which are strictly forbidden on the Sabbath." On another occasion he bitterly complains that we are terrible sinners and "are mixing with the *goyim* and imitating their actions, we are bent to study their language grammatically and we are even spending money to acquire this knowledge;

and at the same time we neglect the study of the Hebrew language." Yet, he himself wrote most of his works, including this complaint, in Arabic.

Another prominent Karaite author who lived in Jerusalem in the second half of the tenth century was Sahl b. Maṣliah ha-Cohen. In his great zeal for Karaism he made several trips to other places in order to spread the doctrines of his sect. He likewise wrote a polemical tract in Hebrew against Saadia Gaon, but he was especially bitter in his disputes with the Rabbanite leader Jacob b. Samuel, who evidently lived in Fustat, Egypt. He also wrote a *Sefer ha-Mitswot*, where he reports that in his period Karaites from various places find refuge in Jerusalem, many of them hailing from Persia, and their women wail and lament in the Hebrew, Persian and Arabic languages.

We come now to the most prominent Karaite Bible commentator, Yefet b. Ali, who was born in Basra, Irak, but resided in Jerusalem during this period, where he probably died. He was a very prolific writer, having translated all the twenty-four books of the Bible into Arabic and commented on them very fully, partly at least in two versions. His commentaries were very popular among Karaites, and even some Rabbanite authors used them, for example, Abraham ibn Ezra who cites him rather frequently. Yefet's commentaries afford much valuable material for the history of the older Karaite literature and theology. Unfortunately, of the many manuscripts extant in the Libraries of Leningrad, London, Oxford, Paris, Berlin and Leyden, only very few have been edited.

During the same period, that is, in the second half of the tenth century, there lived in Jerusalem the celebrated Karaite lexicographer and philologist, David b. Abraham al-Fasi, as, I believe, I have proved in the Introduction to my edition of his Hebrew-Arabic Dictionary of the Bible. This dictionary was abridged by Levi, the son of Yefet b. Ali, himself a prominent scholar.

At the end of the tenth and the beginning of the eleventh centuries, there flourished in Jerusalem the eminent Karaite teacher Joseph ben Noah, who was the head of an Academy, attended, according to a report, by seventy learned men — evidently a round number, in imitation of the Geonic school in Palestine which had seventy *ḥaberim* (member-scholars), also known as the Sanhedrin. Joseph was a very pious man; the rabbinic authority Ali b. Israel Alluf speaks of him as a "servant devoted to God, attired in sackcloth (an ascetic), at the same time searching and investigating the truth in order that he may more firmly believe in it." His comprehensive commentary on the Pentateuch was later abridged by his disciple, the celebrated grammarian Abu'l-Faraj Harun, who also cites his work on Hebrew grammar.

This disciple became the head of the Karaite Academy in Jerusalem after Joseph b. Noah's death, in the first half of the eleventh century. Abu'l-Faraj Harun was the most important Hebrew grammarian among the Karaites. He was highly thought of also by Rabbanite scholars, such as Jonah ibn Janaḥ, Judah ibn Bal'am, Moses ibn Ezra and Abraham ibn Ezra, who refer to him anonymously as "the Grammarian from Jerusalem," (*ha-Medakdek ha-Yerushalmi*). Abu'l-Faraj Harun's most important work is his great philological treatise in Arabic, bearing the title *The Comprehensive Work on the Roots and Subdivisions of the Hebrew Language*. Manuscripts and fragments of this work are found in the Leningrad Library, and, as my friend Professor Kokowzeff told me, it comprises more than 1,200 pages. The work was finished, according to Abu'l-Faraj's own statement, in August, 1026. An abridgement of this work, made by the same author, is being edited by Kokowzeff.

Another prominent disciple of Joseph ben Noah was the

blind philosopher and theologian Joseph ben Abraham, euphemistically called *ha-Roeh* [or *al-Baṣīr* as in Arabic (=סגי נהור)]. His *Book of Investigation*, a kind of *Sefer ha-Mitswot*, was finished in 1036. His other two works, *Kitab al-Muhtawi* (Book of Comprehensiveness) and *Kitab al-Tamyīz* (Book of Distinction) were translated from Arabic into Hebrew and are devoted to philosophical speculations. He is inclined to follow the doctrines of the rationalists among the Arab philosophers, called Mu'tazilites, that the freedom of the will is a certainty and that man possesses the power to determine his own actions, for otherwise it would be unthinkable that he should be punished for actions not in his control. Joseph al-Basir did not develop any new system of philosophy, but his works are important as containing a full discussion of the rationalist doctrines of this early period. Both Abu'l-Faraj Harun and Joseph al-Basir died about the middle of the eleventh century. Manuscripts in the Library of the Jewish Theological Seminary were dictated by this blind Karaite philosopher in 1048.

A very prominent disciple of these two scholars was Joshua b. Judah, known by his Arabic name Abu'l-Faraj Furkan ibn Asad. He wrote a long commentary on the Bible in Arabic in 1050, and four years later he made an abridgement of it. Some of his ethical and philosophical treatises were translated into Hebrew by two of his disciples during his lifetime. He was a man of great learning and was very well acquainted with rabbinic literature, wherefrom he cites on many occasions. He was rationalistic in his views, like his teacher, Joseph al-Basir, and was opposed to the theory of *Rikkub*, which regards man and wife as one body (cf. Gen. 2.24: והיו לבשר אחד), and according to which distant relatives of the husband were prohibited to marry those of the wife and vice versa. On one occasion he states that he asked an intelligent European Jew what was the opinion of his countrymen about several tales and *aggadot* found in the rabbinic literature which regard God in anthropomorphic light, and the reply was that they were all Divine (מפי הגבורה). But some Jews were embarrassed by such *aggadot*, having learned the views of the "Scholars of the Unity of God," evidently referring to Karaite scholars who followed the Muʿtazilites, who called themselves "the People of Unity and Justice."

The last Karaite scholar of note in Jerusalem towards the end of the eleventh and the beginning of the twelfth centuries was Ali b. Suleiman. His was the work of a compiler of the productions of earlier Karaite scholars. Thus he made a Compendium of Levi ben Yefet's Abridgment of David b. Abraham al-Fasi's *Dictionary of the Bible*, but he also utilized for it the works of other grammarians, such as Hayyuj and Abu'l-Faraj Harun, and was already fully acquainted with the triliteral theory of Hebrew roots. He similarly compiled a commentary on the Pentateuch from Abu'l-Faraj Harun's abridgment of Joseph ben Noah's commentary.

With the arrival of the crusaders in Jerusalem in 1099 the great Karaite center in the Holy City came to an end. Even after the reconquest of the city by Saladin in 1187, the Karaite community in Jerusalem remained quite insignificant; it ceased to be the outstanding intellectual center that it had been during the tenth and eleventh centuries. Some of the Karaite residents went to Egypt, others settled in Constantinople, where they strengthened the sectarian movement.

A New Tenth Century Reference to the Jews Praying at the Temple Site in Jerusalem

Paper read in the Oriental Club of Philadelphia
Nov. 12, 1936.

In the *Memorandum on the Western Wall* which Doctor Cyrus Adler prepared for the Special Commission of the League of Nations on behalf of the Jewish Agency for Palestine, he cites only three references to the Jews praying at the Temple site, which go back to the tenth century. The most interesting among them is that of the Karaite Salmon ben Yeruhim, a younger contemporary of Saadia, who resided in Jerusalem for many years. The passage is taken from his Commentary on Ps. 30.10 and reads as follows:

"As is known, Jerusalem was under the rule of the Romans (or Greeks of Christian Byzantium) over 500 years, so that the Jews were not able to enter the city, and anyone who was discovered entering it was slain. When by the grace of the God of Israel the Greeks had departed and the reign of Ishmael became manifest, the Jews were given permission to enter Jerusalem and to sojourn there. The courts of the House of God were given over to them, and they were praying there for some time. When the ruler of Ishmael heard of the unseemly conduct of the Jews in that city, of their wine drinking and intoxication, he commanded that they be confined to one of the gates of the Temple site to pray there, but they were not prevented from visiting the other gates as well. This lasted for some years. However, as the Jews persisted in their evil deeds, there arose against us one who expelled us from that quarter likewise. Whereupon the Christians are now contriving against us through various schemes to drive us out from Jerusalem and separate us entirely from it. But I trust in the grace of the God of Israel that their wish will not be fulfilled," etc.

While Salmon's accusation of the Jewish community in Jerusalem for unseemly conduct was no doubt greatly colored by his intense opposition to rabbinic Jewry and his great intolerance, and should, therefore, be taken with some reservation, he seems to speak as an eyewitness of the political conditions of the Jews in Jerusalem prevailing in his day.

Now, this report of the friendly attitude of the Arabs toward the Jews in the Holy City is corroborated in a passage which I found in the Hebrew-Arabic Dictionary of the Bible of the Karaite lexicographer David b. Abraham al-Fasi, a contemporary of Salmon ben Yeruhim. Thus, in his interpretation of Isaiah 16.4: "Let mine outcasts dwell with thee, Moab; be thou a cover to them from the face of the spoiler," יָגוּרוּ בָךְ נִדָּחַי מוֹאָב הֱוִי סֵתֶר לָמוֹ מִפְּנֵי שׁוֹדֵד; he takes Moab as referring to the Arabs, and he interprets the prophetic significance of the verse as follows: "Let my outcasts, that is the children of Israel who were exiled from their native land, dwell with thee, O Moab, be a shelter to them from the face of the spoiler, meaning the Romans who destroyed the Second Temple and inflicted upon the Jews a heavy punishment, for since the rule of Ishmael was established, Israel has found great ease under the shelter and protection of the Arabs, then they succeeded in entering Jerusalem in order that they may pray opposite the Temple (תֿם אצאבו סביל ללד כֿול אלי אלקדס ליצלּו בחדֿא אלהיכל). For this and similar favors the prophet said: O Moab, be a shelter to them!"

I am inclined to think that both Karaite authors refer to the same situation of the Jews prevailing under the Arab rule in Jerusalem in their days, that is in the second half of the tenth century.

It may be of interest to add here that Mann in his work, *The Jews in Egypt and Palestine under the Fatimid Caliphs*, cites another reference from that period: that after the conquest of Palestine by the Arabs their rulers were favorably inclined toward the Jews, and when they entered Jerusalem, the Jews were entrusted with the task of keeping the Temple site clean and were permitted to pray at its gates without interference.

These friendly relations of the Arab rulers with the Jews of Jerusalem a thousand years ago are especially significant in view of the present friction between the Arabs and the Jews in Palestine.

An Ethiopic Book of Magic[1]

Magic, greatly in vogue in ancient times when it formed an inseparable part of the religious life of the primitive community, continued to play an important role in every-day life also at a much later period and throughout the Middle Ages, despite the frowning upon and admonitions against occult practices by the representatives of the official religion. In fact, we frequently find that many magic beliefs have survived and become part and parcel of later religious systems which had supplanted the simple faith of the primitive man. Thus the study of occult literature helps us to trace the origin of such beliefs when compared with the religious practices described in the literature of ancient times.

Such a combination of the cult of magic with Christianity is amply illustrated by the Ethiopic book *Lifāfa Sedek*, or *Bandlet of Righteousness*, edited with an English translation by Sir E. A. Wallis Budge, which has recently appeared in Luzac's Semitic Text and Translation Series. It is named *Lifāfa Sedek*, from the Arabic root لفّ, to wrap, to bandage, because the magical compositions contained therein were inscribed on a strip of linen or parchment which was wound around the body of the deceased on the day of burial, and this was supposed to protect it from all evil and helped it to pass safely into heaven.

While this book "contains in much-abbreviated and succinct form all the essential elements of the *Book of the Dead* as found in the Recension which was in use in Egypt during the Graeco-

[1] *The Bandlet of Righteousness* an Ethiopian *Book of the Dead*. The Ethiopic text of the *Lefāfa Ṣedeḳ* in facsimile from two manuscripts in the British Museum. Edited with an English Translation by Sir E. A. Wallis Budge, Kt. etc. (Luzac's Semitic Text and Translation Series, Vol. XIX). London: Luzac & Co. 1929. Pp. XV, — 140 — pl. 67.

Roman period" (p. 2), it is the Virgin Mary to whom we really owe its revelation. "Her grief and tears and sorrow for the sufferings which she imagined her kinsfolk would be forced to undergo in the Lake or River of Fire won the compassion and help of her Son, the Word: and he did not rest until God the Father had dictated to Him the secret and magical names in the Book which He had composed before Christ was born in flesh" (p. 6). We see, then, that the book is supposed to have been written by God Himself (p. 61) "with the special object of preserving the bodies of the dead from mutilation, from the attacks of devils, and from the awful River of Fire in hell, and enabling their souls to attain to everlasting life and health and well-being in the kingdom of heaven" (p. 17).

The idea of the River of Fire Wallis Budge traces to the Egyptian *Book of the Dead* (p. 30), and it must not be confused with the נהר דינור, mentioned in Dan. 7, 10,[2] which is not destined for the punishment of the wicked, but flows before the throne of עתיק יומין, and is, according to Midrash Rabbah,[3] the place wherefrom the newly created angels emerge and whereto they return. However, the Lake of Fire as a place of punishment is mentioned in the New Testament, where we read, "And whosoever was not written in the book of life was cast into the lake of fire."[4]

Of special interest is the editor's analysis of this work, as well as his comparisons with other mystical treatises and particularly with the Egyptian *Book of the Dead*. Thus the allusion to the Seal of Solomon ("And if they (i. e. the priests) shall make at the bier (or tomb) the sign of the Seal of Solomon thrice with this book, after he is buried, the angels shall conduct him in through the gates of life") is rather interesting (see pp. 32 f. and 63). The efficacy of the Seal or Ring of Solomon, and also

[2] Cf. Hagigah 13b.

[3] Gen. Rabbah 78 and Ex. Rabbah 15.

[4] Rev. 20, 15.

the manner in which Ashmodai, the king of the devils, was captured by its means are related at length in the Talmud.[5]

In this connection it is to be regretted that the editor's only source reference for the Talmud is Eisenmenger's *Entdecktes Judenthum*, published in Königsberg in 1711, a strongly biased and decidedly anti-Jewish work which has been used by anti-Semites as their main source of information. This work was characterized by G. Dalman in the following terms: "Das Hauptwerk Eisenmengers, sein *Entdecktes Judenthum*, hat die von ihm vohl beabsichtlichen guten Wirkungen nicht haben können weil es sowenig eine Darstellung des Judentums war als eine kritiklose Sammlung alles Hässlichen und Aberglaubischen aus den christlichen Literatur aller Richtungen und Zeiten für eine Characteristik des Christentums gelten konnte. . . Dass auch theologische Publicationen der letzten Jahre es noch als Quelle citieren, gericht unserer Zeit nicht zur Ehre."[6]

The edition is based on two MSS. found in the British Museum, both given in photo-lithographic reproductions. The plates are very clear and easy to read, and the cross-references in the translation to the pagination of the folios of the original (MS. A) materially help to locate and verify any given passage in the text. Yet the fact that "the numbers of the folios in the translation are those of the folios of the manuscript, whilst those given in the photo-lithographic reproduction begin only with the first folio of the text" (p. XIV), thus fol. 2a of the translation is fol. 1a of the text, may cause some confusion at first. Judging from a few passages taken at random, the translation gives a good idea of the text. An Appendix, containing a vision and prayers to the Virgin Mary and other cognate material, is followed by a complete Index, which also includes all the sacred names mentioned in the book. The volume is beautifully gotten up, and is certainly an important addition to the Ethiopic, as well as to the occult literature.

[5] Gittin 68a f.

[6] *Realencyklopädie f. protestant. Theologie u. Kirche*, V. 277.

Judah Halevi

JUDAH BEN SAMUEL HA-LEVI, known by his Arabic name Abu'l-Hasan al-Lawi, was born in Toledo, southern Castile, between 1080 and 1086 — so various scholars assume, for neither the date of his birth nor of his death is definitely known. This was about the time when the city of Toledo was conquered by the Christian king, Alphonso VI. Although the city remained Arab in language and culture for a long time after this, it exerted considerable influence upon the civilization of Christendom. The Jews had been well treated in Toledo by the Mohammedan emirs, and continued to be so treated by the Christian king. Accordingly, the youth of Judah Halevi was not embittered or saddened by Jewish persecutions, as was the lot of many Jewish scholars in the Middle Ages.

Judah's father, Samuel, was a well-to-do man and had amply provided for the education of his son both in religious and secular matters. A very able student, Judah was sent to Lucena, in Moslem Spain, a Jewish cultural center, where he studied Talmud at the school of the celebrated Rabbi Isaac al-Fasi (died in 1103), and enjoyed the companionship of Joseph ibn Migash, Isaac al-Fasi's successor, and Baruch al-Balia, the philosopher. Very sensitive and a poet by nature, Judah, at the age of fourteen, wrote his first poem which has been preserved, written in honor of the old scholar Isaac al-Balia and his son Baruch, on the occasion of the birth of a son to the latter. Following the custom of Jewish scholars of that period, he chose medicine as his profession, in order to avoid making a living from his Hebrew and Talmudic training. So the celebrated Hebrew philologist Jonah ibn Janaḥ had acted before him and

Moses Maimonides and his son Abraham Maimonides after him. It may be added in passing that, while Moses Maimonides was the greatest rabbinic authority of his time, he never occupied a rabbinical post, having practised medicine for his livelihood, though rabbis from many countries sent to him their difficult questions in religious law for final decision.

After receiving a thorough training in the various branches of Hebrew lore as well as in the scientific and philosophic learning of the Arabs, Judah Halevi returned to Toledo, the town of his birth, with the intention of settling there. He devoted himself to the art of medicine and acquired so large a practice that in a letter to a friend he complained of a lack of leisure and calm. However, the more spacious cultural atmosphere of Mohammedan Spain lured him, and he finally settled in the city of Cordova, a great center of Arabic and Jewish culture in Spain. There he reestablished himself as physician and made many friends among the greatest scholars and sages of his age. Little is known of his private life except that he was respected in his community and happy in his home life. He had one daughter, to whose little son, Judah, he was deeply attached. He mentions them both in one of his passionately moving poems.

It was in Cordova that his poetic genius developed to so high a degree that it elicited the following praise from his older contemporary Moses ibn Ezra: "A star rose from Castile, destined to illumine the world." He wrote both secular and sacred poems, the latter numbering about a thousand, of which more than three hundred have been adopted into the liturgy. No chronology of Judah Halevi's poetry is available, but the general assumption is that the material for his singing in his earlier period was secular. It was then that he sang of "the daughter of the vine kindled with the flames of love, cold like snow in the hand of him that holds her, but burning within him like fire." And when, before the age of twenty-four, he was chided for associating with the "vine-daughter," he playfully replied: "How can I despise the *kad* (jug) when my years have not yet reached *kad* (24)."

The genial and sociable nature of Judah Halevi demanded and made friends. In this respect he was quite different from Solomon ibn Gabirol, his predecessor, who was a great poet but lacked the gentle art of friendship and died very young, at the age of thirty-seven. In the four volumes of Halevi's poetry edited and published by Dr. Brody, the poems dedicated to friendship occupy a bulky volume; and many of these poems were most likely written in his early period. "My heart," he exclaimed, "is a holy ark for friendship." He was very sad and dejected at the departure of a friend. The expression *Nedod*, wandering, departure, is frequently mentioned in his verses:

> We know thee, Wandering, from youthful days;
> The stream of weeping is an ancient stream.

Some of these poems were written on occasions of birth, marriage and death in the circle of his friends; and some are of a kind called in Hebrew *Shire Ke'arah*, plate-poems, for it was the custom at that time to present a newly-married couple with a plate inscribed with some appropriate and humorous quatrain. Many of his early poems have love for their theme:

> My law is love, and I to her belong;
> I drew her perfumed breath when I was young.

There is a sensuousness in some of his love-poems, reminiscent of the Song of Songs; but he strikes a truer and deeper note in his sad and more longing moods:

> Would that, after my death, unto mine ears should come
> The sound of the golden bells upon thy skirts. . .
> From my grave I would ask of your love and of your peace.

Unusually beautiful are some of his short poems, as the one where the poet describes a tender devotion hovering over the two worlds of dream and wakefulness, and one is the fulfillment of the other:

> Awake, O my love, from your sleep,
> Your face as it wakes let me view;
> If you dream someone kissing your lips,
> I'll interpret your dreaming for you.

A sensitive soul like Judah Halevi's could not be long satisfied with material success and earthly joys. A period of self-examination and doubt arrived, and he began to sing of the vanity of carnal pleasures and of the folly of material possessions. He made an account of the relations of his soul to her Maker. He would have her "shake off Time's follies like birds shaking off night's drops." He maintains that

> The servants of Time are slaves of slaves;
> The servant of God — he alone is free!
> Therefore, when each man sues for his portion,
> "My portion is God," saith my soul.

God is now one of his main themes. He proclaims the omnipresence of God in the works of creation, and His nearness to those that call upon Him:

> When I went forth to meet Thee,
> Thou didst go forth to meet me!

Or he calls out:

> If I could only see Him in a dream,
> Eternally I'd sleep and never wake.
> If within my heart His face appeared,
> I would never turn my eyes to look outside.

Israel is his second great theme. Sometimes it is pity that streams forth out of our poet's heart:

> Oh you curtains of Solomon,
> How you have changed in the tents of Kedar! (Arabs)
> All your beauty and glory are gone!

Sometimes he sees the utter hopelessness of his people everywhere on the face of the earth, and cries out: "Is there a place East or West where we may feel secure?" At other times he seeks to comfort his people: "Let us not despair though suffering in pain. We are forever, and will not cease as long as day and night do not cease." And sometimes again, particularly in his poems written during the wars between Christianity and Islam — which he called "At a Time of Distress and War" — he fathoms with uncanny clarity the depth of the tragedy of Israel in war-time, of a people lying between the marching legions and the first to be trampled under their spurred hoofs, a tragedy only too familiar to us in the present world struggle:

> Between the armies of the Cross and Crescent,
> My army, crushed, is wholly evanescent,
> The army of Israel.
> When they go forward to the battlefield,
> 'Tis we that fall when they are forced to yield,
> 'Tis always so in Israel.
> Whenever the horns to martial sport resound,
> A doom of death and ruin falls around
> The tents of Israel.

But the highest expression of Judah Halevi's genius was voiced in his passionate love for Zion, as if all the longing accumulated in the Jewish heart for eleven centuries burst forth in him. Zion was to our poet the home of the Divine Presence, the Jerusalem below, whose gates open up to the gates of Jerusalem above, the classical place of that mystic contact with divinity which he always sought. It was the historic past, with all its glory and grandeur which was Jerusalem; it was its desolate present, the air of which was still full of *Ḥayye Neshamot*, soulful life, and the dust and the ruins which still carried for him a pure perfume; it was also its future, for Judah Halevi sincerely believed that the redemption of Zion was near. All these feelings, in addition to a deep and all-dominating love, converge to a burning point in his great poem *Zion, halo tish'ali* (Zion, wilt thou not ask?), perhaps the greatest poem in the Hebrew language since Jeremiah and the Psalms.

It begins with the salutation:

Zion, wilt thou not ask if peace be with thy captives,
That seek thy peace — that are the remnants of thy flocks?
From West, East, North, South, from far and near,
Accept greetings, O Zion,
And also the greetings of that captive of desire
Who sheds his tears like the dew of Hermon
And would fain drop them on thy mountains.

Then, musing over the glories of the past, the poet exclaims:

O who will make me wings, that I may fly afar,
And lay the ruins of my cleft heart among thy cleft hills.
The life of souls is the air of thy land, and of pure myrrh
The grains of thy dust, and honey from the comb — thy rivers.
Sweet would it be unto my soul to walk naked and barefoot
Upon the desolate ruins where thy holiest dwellings were;
In the place of thine Ark where it is hidden, and in the place
Of thy cherubim which dwell in thine innermost recesses.

Such intense love for the Holy Land, so passionately expressed, must translate itself into action, and Judah Halevi contemplates a pilgrimage to Zion. But before setting forth on his journey he writes his famous work, popularly known as *Kuzari*, in defence of the Jewish religion and against the philosophical doctrines current in that period. The work was written in Arabic, and its apologetic character could be seen from the title of the original: *Kitab al-Hujjati wa'l-Dalili fi Nasri'l-Dini'l-dhalili*, which could be rendered into English as "The Book of Proof and Demonstration in Aid of a Faith held in Condemnation."

Halevi begins his work thus: "I was asked what I have to say in answer to the arguments of philosophers, unbelievers and those who profess other faiths against our religion." But instead of working out his ideas systematically, he put them in the form of a dramatic dialogue between Bulan, the first King of the Khazars to embrace Judaism, and a Jewish sage, or *Ḥaber*. The story of the conversion of the Khazars on the Volga River to Judaism in the eighth century, was fresh in the memory of the Jews in Spain, for Ḥasdai ibn Shaprut, the Jewish statesman and patron of learning, who had lived in the tenth century, corresponded with Joseph, the last king of the Khazars, and received an account of the circumstances of their conversion. This historical fact is utilized by the author very skilfully. While the Jews were dispersed and degraded among the nations and the Jewish faith assailed by the followers of its daughter religions and by an unbelieving philosophy, their despised faith won over a king and his people, so powerful, that they proved invincible to the armies of the Persians and Arabs.

The story of the conversion as told by the author reads as follows. King Bulan had a dream, wherein an angel told him that his intentions were pleasing to God, but his deeds were not. His endeavors to be faithful to his religion and piously perform the sacrifices in the temple only led to the repetition of the dream. The king was greatly troubled and consulted a philosopher about his belief, and the latter said to him: "God does not know the particular or the individual, for the individual constantly changes, whereas God's knowledge never changes. Hence God does not know the individual man and, needless to say, he does not hear his prayer. When the philosophers say God created man, they use the word *created* metaphorically, in the sense that God is the cause of all causes, but not that he made man with purpose and intention." The king found no comfort in this and similar statements of the philosopher, for the laws of the universe, as conceived by him, had no interest in standards of human conduct and no concern for the miseries of mankind. The king then said, I will ask the Christians and the Mohammedans. I need not inquire of the Jews, for their low condition is sufficient proof that the truth cannot be with them. But when he heard that both the Christians and the Mohammedans ultimately based their respective faiths on the facts of Jewish history and the teachings of Jewish prophets, he sent for a Jewish sage to hear what he had to say. The questions and arguments, probings and clarifications, between the king and the sage, the *Ḥaber*, constitute the main body of the *Kuzari*.

In essence this work is a rationalized exaltation of Israel and the teachings of Judaism, its sacred language, and the glorious land of its people's ancestors. As the original title of the book indicates, the primary aim of Judah Halevi was to instil courage into the hearts of his people at a time when the crusaders marched to the Holy Land and washed their roads with Jewish blood. Despised and humiliated, Israel is still the people to whose chosen sons God revealed Himself. Reduced and impoverished, Hebrew is still the language of beauty once used by prophets and Psalmists. Wasted and desolate, Palestine is still the land of prophecy and man's experience of God. "But are you not like a dead body now?" asks the king. "No," replies the sage, "not a body, but scattered bones, and yet possessing a spark of life. Not dead, but dangerously ill, and yet with a firm faith that the great miracle of revitalization will happen. . . . We suffer more than any other nation, because Israel is to the nations what the heart is to the limbs of the body; and the heart always feels and suffers more. But suffering is no reason for contempt. . . . The light of God falls only on humiliated souls."

In one of his poems, Judah Halevi says: "Let not Greek wisdom beguile thee, for it hath no fruits, only flowers." This opposition to the metaphysical speculations of Graeco-Arabic philosophy is voiced in the greater part of the *Kuzari*. Since Saadia, and particularly since the works of the celebrated Arab physician and philosopher Ibn Sina (979 — 1037) reached

Spain, a rationalistic tendency had set in to test religious values in the crucible of reason, and to seek to harmonize faith and science. Halevi took as his motto the famous verse of Ben Sirah: "Search not what is too high for thee, nor examine what is beyond thy grasp; endeavor not to know what is hidden, nor investigate what is concealed from thee; study what is within thy mastery, but meddle not with that which is secret." He tried to show that metaphysical speculation and independent reasoning on such difficult matters as God and creation are after all more or less guess-work, and cannot be made the bases of religion except for those who have nothing better. The Jews fortunately have a surer foundation all their own. They have a genuine and indisputable tradition. History is the only true science and the source of truth; not speculation, which is subjective, and can be employed with equal plausibility in favor of opposite doctrines. True history and tradition in the case of the Jews goes back ultimately to first-hand knowledge from the very source of all truth. The prophets of Israel constituted a higher species, as much superior to the ordinary man as the ordinary man is to the lower animal, and these prophets received their knowledge direct from God. In principle, Judah Halevi agreed with the other Jewish philosophers that true reason cannot be controverted. He differed with them in the concrete application of this abstract principle. He had not the same respect as Maimonides for the actual achievements of the unaided human intellect, and an infinitely greater respect for the traditional beliefs of Judaism and the biblical expressions taken in their obvious meaning. Hence he did not feel the same necessity as Maimonides to twist the meaning of Scriptural passages to make them agree with philosophical theories.

According to this view, Judah Halevi did not find it necessary, as did the philosophers and speculative theologians, painfully to prove the existence of God. The existence of the Jewish people and the facts of their wonderful history were more eloquent demonstrations than any that logic or metaphysics could muster. He drew a sharp line between the God of the philosophers and the God of the prophets. The former is transcendent, unconcerned in the affairs of men; the other reveals Himself and hears human prayers and sees human tears. The former is an object of knowledge, and a mistake about the deity is only like an astronomic miscalculation; the latter is loved and worshipped and is a pattern for human living, an ideal for conduct, a cause for self-sacrifice and martyrdom. The former is *Elohim*; the other is *Adonai*. "What a difference between the God of Abraham and the God of Aristotle!" he exclaimed. Thus Halevi showed the limitations of reason; even in the realm of matter the mind has proven itself a small and weak lantern, and "there is more in heaven and earth and sea that the philosopher does not know" — words strangely reminiscent of Shakespeare's lines:

> There are more things in heaven and earth, Horatio,
> Than are dreamt of in your philosophy.

Thus Halevi likewise upholds the Jewish sanctities and stirs in his people a sense of national dignity in the midst of a hostile and mocking world. The *Kuzari* ends with the words: "Jerusalem can be rebuilt only when Israel yearns for it to such an extent as to embrace her stones and kiss her dust."

He finished this work about 1140. His wife having died, he decided to fulfill his passionate longing for Zion. He bade farewell to his only daughter, to his grandson Judah, to his numerous friends and admirers, and started on his journey. Various communities in Spain competed with one another in doing honors to their beloved poet as he traveled through them. Then he sailed in a small wooden bark, which he humorously described as a wooden coffin where he was buried alive, where he could sit but not stand, lie down but not stretch his feet, and yet where the wings of his song stretched wider than ever:

> Rise, ship, seek the land where chambers are for God Himself.
> Hasten, fly, God's hand will carry thee;
> And tie thy wing to the wing of the dawn.

After a stormy voyage, Judah Halevi landed in Egypt where, in Alexandria and later in Damietta, men great in learning and leadership came to greet him and invited him to stay, for in Egypt too the *Shekinah* revealed itself and God's voice was heard. But our poet refused to exchange the place where the divine spirit had its home for a place which it only visited, and he resumed his journey to Zion. Did he reach Jerusalem? Unfortunately, all footprints now disappear. Some historians trace him to Syria, and Dr. I. Zinberg ventures the opinion on the basis of some evidence that Halevi returned to Spain where he soon died. Only legend gives a fitting end to a journey of such intense and passionate yearning: he did arrive in Jerusalem, and while kissing the sacred soil and muttering his poem: "Zion, wilt thou not ask?" an Arab horseman rode by and stabbed him to death with his spear. Legend seems to know the fate of too great a longing.

Adolph Sutro

Civic Leader and Bibliophile

THE ABORTIVE German revolution of 1848 and the reaction which followed it brought to the shores of the United States a number of Jewish immigrants who, either themselves or their descendants, became leaders in science, finance, industry, philanthropy, and other fields of human endeavor. Suffice it to mention here only a few of them: the Lehman family, the Loeb family, the Straus brothers, Dr. Abraham Jacobi, Prof. Albert A. Michelson, Justice Louis D. Brandeis, and others. To this distinguished group of early German-Jewish immigrants, who have brought glory to their adopted country and have fully repaid the freedom and wide opportunities they found here, belongs also Adolph Heinrich Joseph Sutro, of whose life and activities I shall give you here a few details.

Adolph Heinrich Joseph Sutro was born April 29, 1830, in Aix-la-Chapelle, the German Aachen, capital of the district of that name in Rhenish Prussia. He was one of eleven children born to an old German-Jewish family, distinguished for its thrift, industry and integrity. He was educated in his native town and at some of the best polytechnic schools in Germany. His father had extensive woolen mills in Aachen, and at the age of sixteen Adolph had to leave school and assume supervision of his father's business. Shortly thereafter Adolph was entrusted with the establishment of a similar business at Memel, East Prussia. When his father died, in 1847, the management of the business passed into the hands of Adolph and his brother.

But a year later the revolution of 1848 had a bad effect on the Sutro firm. The family was impoverished, so Mrs. Sutro decided to migrate to the United States with her eleven children. In the fall of 1850, they landed in New York, and later settled in Baltimore, Maryland.

It was about that time that the gold rush in California was at its height. The twenty-year-old Adolph readily grasped its meaning and was among the first to take passage on a sailing vessel bound for the port of San Francisco. After a voyage of several months, he finally arrived there on November 21, 1851. His sole fortune was youth, health, hope, courage, ambition and indomitable energy. He went into business on the water front, and for nine years he worked hard in what is called petty trade: buying, selling, keeping a limited supply of the best cigars and tobacco, living frugally, with very few comforts and still less recreation.

Mr. Sutro married in 1856, and thereafter his faithful and devoted wife encouraged and assisted him in all his endeavors during the thirty-seven years of their conjugal life. They had two sons and four daughters.

The discovery of the Comstock Lode in Nevada stirred Mr. Sutro from the monotony of a life devoted to domesticity and to the daily routine of retail trade. He visited the Lode for the first time in 1859 and soon thereafter established at Dayton, Nevada, a stamping-mill for the reduction of silver ore, which proved to be very successful. After careful study of the Lode he saw the immediate need of draining and ventilating the mines. Pumping was a costly and hazardous experiment; a depth of 1,500 feet was reached, and a temperature of 110° prevailed in the lower levels. The air was so foul there that the men who inhaled it fainted or fell dead.

The idea of constructing a tunnel for the purpose of draining and ventilating the mines was first expressed in Mr. Sutro's letter published in the *San Francisco Alta* of April 30, 1860. It was called by critics "An infeasible plan," "The audacity of a dreamer!" but despite this criticism, he secured, alone and unaided, the right of franchise to those mines. His subsequent tasks were to obtain and then retain the confidence of capitalists at home and abroad; to maintain contact with political powers in Washington, in London and also in San Francisco; to make frequent land and sea voyages extending over two continents and, at the same time, to watch the progress of work at the mines and even act as their superintendent. When the merits of the enterprise had become fully understood and recognized, there followed even more desperate efforts to maintain it against conspiracies to push Mr. Sutro out in order that others might appropriate the results of his efforts.

The project was carried through, however, exactly as proposed. On February 4, 1865, Sutro chartered The Sutro Tunnel Co., receiving the approval of Congress in the following year. The construction of the shaft of the tunnel which is situated at Sutro, a village in the Carson River valley, was begun on October 19, 1869, and completed in October 1878. Its dimensions were 10 feet in height, 12 feet in width, 20,500 feet in length; with the north and south branches having 3,600 feet in the aggregate, the entire length of the tunnel extended more than five miles; it was 1,600 feet below the surface. Its cost, including interest, amounted to $6,500,000. This was Mr. Sutro's culminating triumph in the face of powerful opposition from various quarters, ridicule in the press and lack of financial support. Rising above these difficulties, he called a meeting of the miners at Virginia City and by an inspiring address, full of confidence, he gained their wholehearted support.

His task accomplished, Mr. Sutro, in 1879, sold his interest in the corporation he had organized for $5,000,000 and returned to San Francisco, his favorite residence. About that time, the economic depression and the "sand-lot agitation" had greatly depreciated the value of real estate. Mr. Sutro did not share the general despair in the city's future and invested heavily in the sand hills of the shorelands, believed by the doubting public to be worthless, as well as in other real estate. He thus became one of the wealthiest men on the Pacific Coast, owning about one-tenth of the area of San Francisco.

The arid acres of the sand hills were improved by Mr. Sutro through piercing the subterranean depths by shafts and pumps and sinking iron pipes through the rocky hills in search of water. The stony structure was blasted and cut into staircases, terraces and walls of lakelike reservoirs. Millions of seedlings were planted, which have grown to sturdy groves skirting the horizon. Sutro Heights became a superb suburb, situated upon a natural, walled promontory, overlooking the beautiful mountains, the Golden Gate, the seal rocks, the sea and the beach. Here Mr. Sutro established his quaint and unique residence, with statuary — copies of celebrated sculpture brought from Europe — set in niches, terraces, flower-beds, parapets, along tree-lined walks and drives.

Mr. Sutro proceeded then to build what is now known as the Sutro Baths. They are located in a wave-worn cove at the foot of the cliffs and consist of a series of basins, located in the rock. They receive water from the ocean's caverns by an intricate system of tunnels and canals, so ingeniously devised as to supply the receptacles with both hot and cold currents and then drain them after use. There are six tanks, the largest being L-shaped, 300 feet long and 150 feet wide at its farthest extremity; another, 75 x 50 feet, is reserved for the use of women and children; and four are 75 x 28 feet; the depth of the water varies from two to eleven feet. All these tanks are walled and floored with creamy concrete, filled or drained as desired. All kinds of paraphernalia are provided for aquatic sports. Five hundred dressing rooms, well ventilated, heated, lighted by electricity, furnished with showers, soap, toweling, bathing suits and all necessary toilet articles, are reached with the aid of spacious elevators and broad staircases that lead also to arcades, pavilions, promenades and corridors, adorned with tropical plants, fountains, flowers, pictures and bric-a-brac collected in foreign travel.

A distinctly noticeable feature of this stupendous establishment is a stage, constructed for the performance of operas, dramas and other public entertainments. The seats, arranged in tiers, form an amphitheatre facing the ocean side of the structure, and are walled with glass of many colors, causing the most fantastic effects by filtering sun-beams. A seating capacity is afforded for 25,000 spectators within the building.

But the crowning glory of Mr. Sutro's achievement was to be a great library, housed in a fine building, constructed on the plan of the British Museum library and supplied with every book needed by scholars for their research. This was to be located in a recess of the hills near the site of the affiliated colleges of the University of California, against a background of pines, cypress and acacia trees. To this project Mr. Sutro gave time, thought and money with unsparing zeal; but his failing health in his last years prevented this, his dearest hope and broadest vision, from being consummated before he died on August 8, 1898. With his life passed the romantic vision of the Sutro Library, but at the time of his death he was said to possess one of the largest private libraries in the world.

Mr. Sutro's aim was to establish in his home city a large research library, similar to those he had seen in the European capitals. To this end, he and his staff of English and German experts began, in 1883, buying many thousands of books in London, on the continent and in Mexico. In 1894, Mr. Sutro was elected Mayor of San Francisco on the Populist ticket, and, in 1895, when he offered a site for the affiliated colleges of the University of California, he included a description of the Sutro Library which he planned to house nearby. In this description, he stated that the Library contained over 200,000 volumes and more than 4,000 incunabula. The latter had come mainly from the Royal State Library at Munich, which had absorbed the libraries of the confiscated monasteries of Bavaria. The Royal State Library had sold Mr. Sutro its duplicates.

After his death, in 1898, the estate was in litigation for many years and the Library was stored in two warehouses: on Battery street and at the Montgomery block. In 1906, the San Francisco earthquake and fire destroyed the Battery Street warehouse, containing more than half of the entire Library and most of the very rare incunabula. The rest of the Sutro Collection, about 100,000 volumes and fewer than fifty incunabula, was given to the State of California in 1913. It was accepted by the Legislature in 1915, to be maintained as a separate branch of the State Library at San Francisco under the terms of the gift. It should be added here, by the way, that both the Sutro Heights and the Sutro Baths became the property of the city of San Francisco after Mr. Sutro's death.

A portion of the Sutro Collection is housed at present in the Sutro Hall of the Free Library of San Francisco, but the greater part of it is found in the cellar of the Library building. However, I was informed last year that the Legislature has finally appropriated the necessary funds to erect a suitable building for housing the entire collection.

The Sutro Collection

Sixteenth Century Books:

Many classical, religious, and controversial works in various European languages.

English:

Pamphlets — about 25,000, dating from 1640, the time of the English Civil War on. Some supposed to be from Lord Macaulay's library.

Drama — Shakespeare, 1 copy of each, 1st (1623), 2nd (1632), 3rd and 4th folio editions. Several hundred English plays from 1630 on.

Manuscript material, deeds, etc., from the vicinity of Stratford-on-Avon.

Mexican:

Large collection of Spanish and Mexican books, pamphlets, newspapers, etc.

Mexican pamphlets — 35,000, among them some covering the period of the Mexican Revolution, around 1820, many of them not available elsewhere.

Official government reports, 1820 — 1865.

California:

No Californiana or Americana, except files of early San Francisco and Sacramento newspapers and several hundred sermons printed in America before 1800.

Judaica and Hebraica:

A great deal of Judaica, especially 19th century publications, many of them very rare, and some Hebraica.

Hebrew and Judaeo-Arabic Manuscripts:

More than 150. Among them 20 Torah scrolls; many Yemenite Bibles, with the Targum and Saadia Gaon's Arabic Version; several copies of *Midrash ha-Gadol* on the Five Books of Moses; many copies of *Mishneh Torah* of Maimonides, and other Hebrew and Judaeo-Arabic works, the oldest among them dating from the 13th century. They are mostly of Yemenite origin, and among them I was fortunate to identify two manuscripts of an old Masoretic Hebrew grammar. This grammar was edited by

Neubauer, who was on the staff of the Bodleian Library in Oxford, on the basis of several manuscripts and published in 1891. When I collated his edited text with that of the two Sutro manuscripts, I found that their text is much more correct and more complete than the Neubauer edition, where several words and even whole lines are missing.

It is really a great pity that the cherished dream of Mr. Sutro to establish an extensive research library on the Sutro Heights, in the vicinity of the University of California, according to his plan, was not realized in consequence of his illness and premature death. In view of the circumstance that the Sutro Heights have not suffered much from the San Francisco earthquake, the entire library would have been preserved, including the priceless collection of 4,000 incunabula, one of the finest in the world.

The Treatise of Maimonides on Health Care

Moses Maimonides, born in Cordova, Spain, in 1135, died in Egypt in 1204, was equally celebrated as religious philosopher, leading legal authority, and noted physician. It was in the latter capacity that he was engaged at the court of the Sultan Ṣalāḥ ad-Dīn, better known as Saladin, in Egypt. He wrote several medical treatises, among them (1) *On Hemorrhoids;* (2) *On Poisons;* (3) *On Sex Hygiene;* (4) *On Asthma;* (5) *Aphorisms of Moses,* largely selected from Galen's works, and (6) a *Treatise on Health Care,* written at the request of the Sultan al-Mālik al-Afḍal, son of Ṣalāḥ ad-Dīn and one of his successors.

The last named treatise, bearing the Arabic title *Fi Tadbīr aṣ-Ṣiḥḥah* is interesting from many view-points. It presents a clear picture of the ideas about personal hygiene as well as dietetics prevalent among the leading physicians in Arabic-speaking countries in the twelfth century. Maimonides is quite emphatic when he speaks of nature as taking care of man's indispositions, blaming the ignorance of some physicians who do not permit nature to take the time necessary for self-help. Accordingly, he stresses the importance of a thorough professional training for physicians, careful personal attention to patients, and medical treatment along such lines as would help the natural forces working for recuperation. Slight indispositions should, whenever possible, be treated without any special help of a physician and without resorting to drugs. His theories Maimonides bases on Galen and Hippocrates, whom he cites pretty often.

The treatise was written in response to the complaints of the Sultan al-Mālik al-Afḍal that he suffers most of the time from constipation and poor digestion and occasional weakness. He is also subject at times to sadness, morbid thoughts, apprehension and fear of death. With the view of giving adequate advice to the Sultan, Maimonides states that he thought it expedient to write four chapters on this subject, which comprise the present treatise. The titles of these chapters are:

(1) "About Health Care in General, as Applied to All People, Briefly Stated."

(2) "About Care of the Sick in General in the Absence of a Physician or Where There is an Unskilled Physician, Whose Knowledge cannot Be Relied Upon."

(3) "Treatment of the Sultan, Especially the Ailments of Which He Complains," and

(4) "Some Paragraphs Comprising Advices Generally Useful for the Healthy and the Sick Alike, under All Circumstances."

I shall give here a translation of the first two chapters which are of particular interest, for they deal with preservation of health in general, advice on diet, and first aid in the event of illness.

It should be mentioned here that the Arabic text was edited by Rabbiner Dr. H. Kroner and published in *Janus* in 1925, with a German translation.

Chapter I

"About Health Care in General, as Applied to All people, Briefly Stated."

The purpose of this chapter is to set down certain rules which are easy to observe, yet very useful for the preservation of health. They are generally followed by the best physicians. To them belongs the principle of Hippocrates: "Continuation of good health depends on being careful of over-eating and of sluggishness." His whole theory of health is thus condensed into two brief rules: "A man should not eat too much, nor should he give up exercise." It is so, for over-eating, i. e. eating to the point of aversion, results in over-stuffing the stomach and stretching it, and when an organ is unduly stretched, its joints become loose and it gets rather weak. The stomach, therefore, is unable to digest this mass of food properly; the result is general sluggishness, laxity of movement, and over-loading with food, especially when followed by excessive drinking, which necessarily brings about over-satiation. It may result either in a serious digestive disturbance which may be fatal, or in a lighter disturbance causing indigestion and other diseases, all depending on the kind of food and the susceptibility of the organs to various diseases. When food is poorly digested in the stomach, the second digestion in the liver as well as the third digestion in the other organs[1] are likewise bad, and this, in turn, helps to develop various kinds of disorders. Hence the statement of Galen: "Whoever wishes to keep healthy should endeavor to avoid poor digestion and not move around too much after meals."

In view of the harm of over-satiation all physicians warn against it, insisting that a person should restrain himself from eating when he has not yet fully satisfied his appetite, thus avoiding the over-loading and stretching of the stomach. All physicians agree that eating a small quantity of food of inferior quality is less injurious than consuming an excessive quantity of superior quality. In the former case, while the appetite is not entirely satisfied, the food is thoroughly digested and the whole body gets the benefit of whatever nourishment it contains, thus strengthening the eliminating forces to throw off the bad portions of this food with little or no injury to the one who eats it. However, when an excessive quantity of food is consumed,

[1] The author probably means by that the assimilation of the food in the body.

be it even carefully prepared bread and the choicest of meat, it could not be thoroughly digested, as we have mentioned above.

With the view of avoiding over-eating, physicians advise against taking many kinds of food at one meal, but the meal should be limited to one kind, so that the food consumed will not be too much and the appetite will be satisfied before reaching full satiation. One will also thus avoid a variety of digestions, for different kinds of food differ in their digestion, each kind in accordance with its nature.

With regard to the quantity of food for one who takes care of his health the opinion of the Servant is that in mild weather one should eat only as much as will not stretch his stomach and as will not overtax it and thereby interfere with its digestion. When the proper quantity is determined, he should choose a food suitable to his nature, causing no belching or thirst, but conducive to cheerfulness and vivacity, and resulting in a gentle disposition, somewhat inclined to softness. This much is an adequate quantity which one should habitually take.

When the weather gets hot, it is advisable to consume less food, for digestion is rather poor during the summer on account of the release of the innate heat. But when the temperature grows colder, one should increase the consumption of food, for digestion is strengthened in winter, the natural heat being preserved in the body owing to closed up pores, and the appetite grows stronger.

Says the Servant, if a person took as good care of himself as he does of his beast which he rides, he would avoid many diseases. No one throws food to his beast recklessly, but he feeds it in accordance with its needs, yet he himself consumes food without any control or measure. One should also take into consideration the moving around of domestic animals and the exercise they get lest they become permanently stiff and perish. He, however, does not do that with himself and does not think of exercising his body, which is the greatest support of lasting good health and a ward against most diseases.

We have mentioned the statement of Hippocrates that "Continuation of good health depends on being careful of sluggishness." Indeed, there is not a thing that could take the place of exercise, for with exercise the natural heat increases and all waste matter is thrown off, while inertness extinguishes the flame of the natural heat, and the superfluities of the body are not eliminated. Even if the food be best in quality and moderate in quantity, exercise would still eliminate the evil effects of much of the harmful conduct in which most people indulge. But not every movement of the body is considered exercise by physicians. Only a vigorous or quick movement, or both combined, could be called exercise. It is with a vigorous movement resulting in change of respiration that a person begins to breathe deeply. A movement stronger than that brings about fatigue, i. e. very strong exercise causes fatigue, which not everybody is able to stand, nor is there a particular necessity in that, for the brief exercise is most beneficial for the preservation of health.

One should exercise on an empty stomach only, and after the excrements (urine and bowels) are thrown off. Exercise should similarly be avoided in excessive heat and excessive cold. The best time for it is early in the morning, after one gets up from his sleep and throws off the excrements, as mentioned. To the general principles for the preservation of good health, recommended by Galen, belongs the following: "Just as movement before eating is altogether beneficial, so is movement after eating quite injurious." Any exercise after meals is quite harmful; by this is meant strenuous exercise, as well as coitus and bath, which is very harmful, especially to those who naturally have thin and narrow veins, and may result in great injury. Yet it is advisable to move around lightly after meals from one end of the room to the other, until the food is well settled at the bottom of the stomach and rests there until digested. Sleep helps digestion, especially with those who are in the habit of sleeping in the day time.

One of the rules of health care is that one should avoid eating soon after he has already eaten, but rather wait until he gets really hungry, the stomach empty, and the saliva begins to accumulate in his mouth. When one is truly hungry, then is the time for a beneficial meal. Neither should one drink unless he is really thirsty. As soon as hunger or thirst is felt one should wait a while, for there is a false feeling of hunger, as well as of thirst, due to a bad secretion which irritates the opening of the stomach. If this feeling subsides, no taking of food is then necessary. If, on the other hand, it increases, the hunger or thirst should be satisfied. Drinking right after the meal is injurious and interferes with digestion, unless one is used to it. It is not advisable to drink during the meal, nor after it, anything but pure cold water, with no admixture to it, as long as the food is in the stomach.

Another rule for the preservation of health is that one should not take an enema for the purpose of removing the residue in the stomach, unless there is special need of its removal, in which case one must proceed with it forthwith. It is then advisable not to eat, nor take a bath, nor have coition, nor sleep, nor do any exercise before the patient is examined and the residue is removed from the stomach. He should likewise get examined after he has done the five things enumerated here.

Among the rules of health-care is also the need of examining the quality of food. One could write a very long chapter on this subject, in which a knowledge of the nature of various kinds of food would be essential. Physicians have written many long treatises on this subject, and necessarily so, because of its great importance. However, for our present purposes we shall limit ourselves to foods commonly used and abundantly found here, and describe their benefits.

Superior foods which should be preferred by all who take good care of their health are: Well prepared wheat bread, meat of one- or two-year old sheep, chickens, heath-cocks, partridges, pigeons, and also yolks of hens' eggs. By well prepared bread is meant that it should be of fully ripened wheat after the superfluous moisture was dried in it, and the wheat must not be too old as to be on the verge of deterioration or begin to sprout. The bread should also have bran, i. e. the husks must not be removed by a sieve; it must be well leavened, well salted, thoroughly kneaded, and baked in an oven. This is called by physicians "well prepared bread," and it makes the best food.

It should be noted that whatever is prepared of wheat besides this bread cannot be considered superior food at all. Indeed, some such preparations are very bad foods, as unleavened bread, and cooked dough, as vermicelli and noodles, called by the Persians "Tutmaj," and cooked flour, as "Ḥarīra"[2] and " 'Aṣīda,"[3] roasted (or fried) dough, as sweet pancakes, and bread moistened with olive oil or any other oil. All these are very bad foods for everybody. Likewise bread baked of white flour, or fine flour, and cooked meat and wheat pounded together cannot be recommended as excellent foods. If they are nourishing, when well digested, these foods require a stomach with a good digestion, and only then are they quite beneficial.

As for the kinds of meats which we have mentioned above, not all of them have the same nature, neither could all be equally recommended. The best kind of meat of cattle is that of sheep grazing in the mountains, one or two years old, and moderately fat. The best part of the animal is its forward part

[2] A soup of flour and milk.

[3] A gruel prepared of flour with butter and honey.

and the meat adhering to the bones, whatever is found in the abdomen being inferior in quality. Similarly all fats are bad, for they satiate, cause indigestion, diminish the appetite, and form a mucous secretion. Also the heads of animals contain more indigestible matter than any other organ. On the other hand, the shanks contain less of this matter and their use as food is not so bad. Lambs, again, abound in refuse matter and there is not much good in them, while suckling kids are good to eat and easy to digest. Meat of fowl is generally lighter than that of cattle and is much easier to digest. The best fowl meat is that which was mentioned above.

Fresh milk is a good food for those in whose stomach it will not sour, nor ferment, nor form flatulence in the region below the loins (below the epigastrium). Galen recommends that a little honey and a pinch of salt should be added to the milk in order to avoid its curdling in the stomach. The best kind of milk is the tenderest, as milk of goats; that of she-camels is good, too. Whatever is prepared of milk, or mixed with it, is very bad, as curdled milk, sweet and sour milk mixed together, and whey. Likewise all that is cooked of milk and in milk is unwholesome as food. Cheese is a very poor and heavy food, except fresh white cheese which is sweet of taste and contains little fat. Galen praises it as a nourishing food. Other kinds of cheese are objectionable, especially old cheese containing much fat. Fresh and melted butter is not a bad food for anybody.

Bees' honey is beneficial for old people, but inadvisable for the young, especially of hot temperament, for it changes into yellow bile. Fish is mostly a poor food, especially for those who possess a moist nature (phlegmatics) and old people. Above all, the fish that has a large body, salted fish, as well as that which frequents bad slimy water and is a viscous fish. On the other hand, fish small of body and white of meat, which acquired a sea taste, and those found in flowing water, as, e. g., the kind called mullet or sardines, they are not unwholesome as food, yet should not be used too much.

It is known among all physicians that the best of all foods is what is generally known as forbidden by the Moslem religion. It combines all the nourishing qualities of food, forming a good, rich, and light food which facilitates and helps digestion, and rids the body of waste matter by discharging urine and perspiration. It has other superior qualities and many virtues enumerated by physicians. However, it is quite useless to talk about a food, the use of which is not permissible; we shall, therefore, refrain from mentioning its kinds and the manner of using it with regard to the preservation of health.[4]

Vegetables generally not wholesome as food are: garlic, onions, leek (related to the onion), radishes, cabbage and egg-plant; people who take care of their health should avoid them. Cucumbers and green melons are not so bad. The yellow cantaloupe is easily digestible, when eaten the first thing in the morning on an empty stomach, having no flow of bad secretion and not containing any bad mixture. It has then a slight cooling effect on the body, throws off the urine and cleans the veins of impurities, it is thus not an unwholesome food. I have mentioned it here, for it is much used by all people.

With regard to fresh fruit it is well to know that whatever grows on trees is generally objectionable as food. Yet some fruit is worse than others; thus, carobs, fruit of the lotus tree, and the medlar are very bad, while figs and grapes are not nearly as bad, in fact almost wholesome; so Galen speaks of figs and grapes as chiefs to all fruit. They are indeed least harmful, yet one should not overtax the blood which is required for digesting all fruit. My statement that whatever grows on trees is objectionable

[4] The author evidently refers in this paragraph to grape-wine and nabīḏ, a beverage made of dates or raisins, the use of which is prohibited by Moslem religion.

as food must not be misunderstood in view of the fact that fruit juices, as well as syrups and confections prepared from fruits, are beneficial as medicine in certain diseases, for the virtue of foods as nourishment is different from their virtue as remedies for diseases; this is quite evident to those who are versed in the medical art.

There is a statement by Galen offering advice to people, and he swears that he is quite emphatic in his advice, in which he prohibits the eating of fruit. He says that every year he used to suffer from fever, so his father advised him to abstain entirely from eating fruit, and that year he was indeed free from fever. Moreover, as long as he lived he ate no fruit, and he swears that since then up to the time he wrote his treatise he had suffered from fever only one day. What he states is true, for summer fruit is the source of fevers. The fact that many people eat this fruit, yet suffer no fever is no proof to the contrary, for change in habits and variety in dispositions bring about different rules. If the Hindu, e. g., ate well prepared bread and mutton, he would surely become ill, and, on the other hand, if one of us limited his diet to rice and fish, as the Hindus always do, he would likewise become ill. However, the purpose of this treatise is not to cite the causes thereof, but to teach that, generally speaking, fruits are unwholesome and should be eaten in moderate quantities, nor should they be mixed with other food in any form. Fruits which act as laxatives, as plums, grapes and figs, are to be consumed before the meal, which is to be taken only after the fruit is emptied from the stomach, while those that act as astringents, as quinces and pears, should be taken after meals in moderate quantities, enough to have their fragrance in the stomach. Just as figs and grapes are the best of fruits, so are peaches and apricots the worst among them. The latter two cannot be digested at all, a residue of waste matter necessarily remaining in the veins mixed with the blood where it eventually ferments, thus being the chief cause for putrid fever.

Dried fruits, such as raisins, dried figs, kernels of pistachio nuts and of dry almonds, are not unwholesome, and they are recommended as beneficial after meals, especially raisins and pistachio nuts which are very good for the liver, and, as Galen likewise said, "A healthy liver is our life!" In a similar manner it is good to take a little of some sweet dessert after the meal, in order to enable the stomach to envelop the food and digest it. This much I thought it advisable to mention in the present chapter, which is sufficient for our purpose.

Chapter II

"About Care of the Sick in General When There is no Physician or When There Is a Physician Whose Knowledge Cannot Be Relied Upon."

People of intelligence know that the medical art is quite indispensable to man, especially to city dwellers who are in the habit of eating very much, and that one cannot get along without a physician at certain times and under certain conditions. For the medical art has three functions: First and most important is the care of the healthy, i. e. to be careful of the health that one possesses so as not to lose it (prophylactic); second is treatment of the sick, i. e. developing the art of restoring lost health, which is known as "the art of healing"; third is the treatment which Galen calls "revitalizing," i. e. treatment of those who do not enjoy good health nor are they ill, as the treatment of convalescents and the aged.

It is thus evident that a man is in need of the treatment of a physician in whatever condition he may be and at all times. However, the need of a physician is greatest during illness, when the absence of a doctor may be dangerous; accordingly, the masses of people think that a physician is needed only in illness, not otherwise. Frequently one becomes ill on a journey, or in a small town where there either is no physician or he is unreliable. Therefore, the Servant thought [it advisable] to outline what should be done in such a case.

I say that Galen had explained to us that formerly all the Greeks, when in doubt about some disease, did not treat it at all, but left the patient to nature, for that is sufficient in curing diseases. Hippocrates, in several places in his works, was profuse in praise of nature, that it is skilful and sagacious enough to do what is necessary and does not need any other curative measures. The physician's function is only to assist nature, nothing else, and to follow its course. Ar-Razi says in one of his famous chapters that when the disease is stronger than the power of resistance of the patient, one cannot hope to save him nor would a physician benefit him in any way. When the power of resistance of the patient is stronger than the disease, then there is no need of a physician at all, for nature will heal him. But when the disease and the resistance to it are equal, then there is need of a physician to aid this resistance, and if he is skilful, he will know how to support nature and assist it, and how to remove its obstacles. However, most physicians greatly err in this matter: they think that they help its power, but they really destroy or hinder it, or interfere with its course. For this reason Aristotle, in his book "On Sense and Things Perceived by the Senses" (*De Sensu et Sensibili*), states that most death cases are due to medicine, because most physicians are ignorant of nature. By "nature" the medical authorities mean in this instance the force which governs the body of animals, whose existence and exact functions are demonstrated in the scientific books treating of the "Science of the Elements." On that account, some kings have engaged a number of physicians, choosing those with an acute mind and long practice, so that by their joint opinion they may be free from error.

From the entire preceding discussion it is quite evident that a patient should be left to nature in the event there is no qualified physician at hand. By "leaving to nature" is meant that he should not take any remedies not usually taken by healthy people and he should not leave off food entirely. Let him drink when thirsty and eat when hungry, and at the time when the patient is accustomed to eat, taking the lightest foods he is in the habit of eating. It is necessary that he should know that even if he had a famous physician, or a number of them, he could not save himself by resorting to drastic remedies except at the advice of a very well trained physician of sound knowledge and widely known experience. Otherwise, one should, in the event of illness, have recourse to mild, not drastic, remedies.

I shall now explain what the drastic remedies are. They are cutting a vein and letting much blood; evacuation by means of strong purgatives, as colocynth marrow and scammony; evacuation through vomiting, as the potent remedies like the two kinds of hellebore plants and the emetic nut (*Nux vomica*); a sharp enema, containing colocynth marrow, sagapenon (medicinal gum), castor oil, and the like; likewise depriving the patient of food entirely and prohibiting him to take any nourishment at all, refraining from drinking water and suffering thirst, or taking very useful medicinal confections (electuaries), as theriac, mithridas, theodoritos, and the like. All these remedies are very drastic, and should be resorted to only at the advice of a physician possessing superior knowledge. All such treatments, if administered at the proper time, may cure the patient at once or shortly thereafter, or save him from death. But if they miss the right time, they may in most cases cause immediate death, or may bring about another disease, resulting in subsequent death. It is, therefore, necessary to beware of them.

The mild remedies are, e. g., bloodletting by cupping the legs or the upper part of the body; softening the bowels with manna, manna water, plums, cherries, violets, refined rose syrup, and the like; inducing to vomit by means of barley water, oxymel, radishes, spinach seed, melon roots, etc.; a mild enema, as in conjunction with barley broth, boiled bran, honey water, rasins alone, and similar remedies. The patient should likewise be on a light diet, taking the usual syrups of sugar or bee honey, barley water, barley gruel, or washed kernels; he may also take a little bread in liquids. In like manner is the treament with healthful remedies, I mean such as are frequently taken by healthy people, as the well known syrups of oxymel, roses, lemon, violets, etc.; also similar juices, as preserves of roses, violets, myrobalan, etc.; likewise taking well cooked mixtures of mild remedies, as licorice, ox tongue, endive seed, orange peel, eryngium, asparagus root, peel of endive root, fennel, lettuce, wild cucumber seed, seed of garden purslane, cucumber seed, melon seed, marshmallow wood and its seed, etc.; also mixed juices prepared of fruits, seeds and blossoms, which are usually taken by healthy people, as is also the juice of tamarind. All these remedies are mild, so if they are effective in some cases, they may cure slight indispositions and in course of time even more serious diseases. On the other hand, if they are ineffective, they would not be fatal, nor would they cause any serious damage. For this reason we find most physicians following this method of treatment in order to be on the safe side.

As for cathartics like hiera, agaric, turbid, and the like, as well as cassia fistula, they are of the intermediate kind. They are neither strong purgatives nor mild laxatives. While cassia fistula may cause distress and at times diarrhea, it is quite reliable. Also agaric is safe as a laxative, yet it may be quite injurious through its acidity (?) and great dryness in cases where there is need of moisture either in the whole body or in one of the limbs. For that reason hiera and triphylla are most of the time quite injurious in fever cases. Hence our caution in taking theriac and mithridates only at the advice of a distinguished physician. But this is the case only with the sick; for the health care of well people medical authorities have recommended to take some theriac every ten days.

However, there are no absolute rules in medical practice, but for every treatment it prescribes there are certain necessary conditions. So physicians recommend taking theriac every ten days as a health measure. Yet it should not be taken in very hot weather, nor by people having a hot temperament or a bad secretion in their stomach, of whatever kind it may be. Similarly is vomiting once or twice a month recommended as a very good health measure. But this, too, is subject to certain conditions: the person should not have a weak chest, nor be disposed to quick congestion in his head, nor be suffering with frequent headaches; neither is vomiting beneficial in very cold weather. In like manner is every medical treatment dependent on certain conditions, as shown here.

We have advised here the use of mild remedies, some of which were mentioned above, in the event there is no skilful physician at hand and one has to follow the suggestion of any physician present. However, this should be done only in case of necessity, for even this type of remedy may be injurious, if the physician is mistaken in determining the nature of the disease. Galen has explained that a patient may be instructed to drink water until he quenches his thirst, his body becomes then moist with perspiration, his constitution soft, his fever ceases, and he fully recovers. But it may happen that a patient is advised to drink water at a time when he should not, and this may result in his death, or in acquiring some chronic ailment from which he will never recover. Thus the conditions should be established under which drinking water is to be permitted or forbidden.

Now, if this is the case with drinking water, how much more should one be careful with other remedies. When the symptoms are conflicting and it cannot be certain whether drinking water should be permitted or not, the patient is to be allowed to drink it, but not excessively.

The case is similar with food: If we are not certain whether the patient should take some food or not eat anything at all, it is advisable to put him on a light diet. And thus should be the treatment when no skilful physician is to be found: one should always follow the habits of the healthy, but take a little less than the usual quantity. Strength is to be always preserved by taking nourishment, either a light diet, such as chicken soup, beef broth, the yolk of a soft boiled egg, and wine for him who can take it, or some heavier food, such as spring chicken and bread. The patient should never neglect sustaining his natural strength by food and his spiritual strength by pleasant odors, warm ones, as musk, amber, and sweet basil in the case of cool diseases, and cool scents, as rose, white lotus, myrtle, and violet in the case of hot (fever producing) diseases. Also quickening the animal strength of the patient by means of musical instruments and cheerful stories, which would delight his soul and set him at ease, telling him anecdotes which would divert him and make him laugh, and by visits of friends whom he would be pleased to see. All this is quite essential in any illness in the absence of a physician, when things are to be arranged in the proper manner.

Medical authorities have advised physicians that whenever possible they should treat a patient with a special diet only, without resorting to drugs. In case one has to use drugs, it is advisable to take first ready made remedies, as dietetic medicines or medicinal foods. If the patient must resort to pure drugs, he should begin first with the weakest of the remedies, and if it is satisfactory, it is quite sufficient; if not, let him proceed to stronger and stronger remedies. In cases which could be treated by simple remedies one should not use any compounds, but if one is obliged to use the latter, those which contain the least number of ingredients should be chosen. One should have recourse to drugs containing many ingredients only in extreme necessity.

Now if these recommendations have been offered with regard to skilful physicians, what should be recommended when there is no physician? One should certainly be very careful not to dare use strong remedies nor to be thoughtless in taking too many drugs. The patient should rather confine himself to the customary weakest remedies. This measure is what we thought advisable to recommend in this matter.

These two chapters of the treatise of Maimonides on Health Care clearly show, I believe, his advanced ideas on preservation of health. It is also interesting to note that Maimonides pays due attention to the influence of the mind on the recuperative powers of the body. Accordingly, the patient must be put in a happy frame of mind in order to hasten his recovery.

MAIMONIDES ON PERSONAL HYGIENE

Since by keeping the body in sound health one walks in the ways of God, a person should shun ways of life that destroy the body and train himself in health restoring habits.

Eat only when you are really hungry and drink when you are thirsty.

A person should never eat until his belly is full, only about three fourths of his fill. Before eating he should walk or work until he gets tired and his body becomes heated; he should then rest a while and eat. It is also good to wash with warm water after he gets tired, then rest a while and eat.

After eating, a person should always remain sitting in his place until his food is digested (settles) in his entrails. Whoever walks or exerts himself right after eating brings illness upon himself.

There are twenty-four hours in the day and night, and a third of them — eight hours — are sufficient for sleep, and the best time for sleep is at the end of the night, so that the eight hours will end in the morning before sunrise, the best time to rise. One should not sleep on his face nor on his back, but on his side. Neither should one sleep right after eating, but wait about three or four hours after the meal. Nor should one sleep in the day time.

There is a general rule for bodily health: Whoever works hard, does not eat to his fill, and keeps his bowels regular — he will be free from sickness and become strong even when he eats poor food. But whoever leads an idle life and does not take exercise, even if he eats the best of foods he will be ill and in poor health. Excessive eating and gluttony is like poison to the human body.

Mohammed's Night Journey from Mecca to Jerusalem and His Subsequent Ascension to Heaven

THE STORY of Mohammed's night journey (*Al-Isra*) from Mecca to Jerusalem is based on a single verse in the Koran, the only one that has direct reference to it. This verse reads as follows:

Praise be unto Him who transported His servant by night from the sacred temple (of Mecca) to the farther temple (of Jerusalem), the circuit of which we have blessed, that we might show him of our signs; for He is the Hearer, the Seer (Koran XVII, 1).

While the verses following this have nothing to do with the journey, the oldest traditions relate that from the temple of Jerusalem Mohammed traveled through the seven heavens. It is generally accepted by Moslem theologians that verse 62 of this Sura which reads:

We have appointed the vision which we showed thee, and also the tree[1] cursed in the Koran, only for an occasion of dispute unto men, and we will strike them with terror; but it shall only increase in them enormous wickedness,

has allusion to his journey to heaven. Another reference to this journey is found by some authorities in the following passage in the Koran (LIII 13–18)

[1] The name of the tree is *al-Zakkum*, and it comes up from the bottom of hell (Koran XXXVII, 60).

He also saw him (Gabriel) another time, by the lote-tree[2] beyond which there is no passing. Near it is the garden of (eternal) abode. When the lote-tree was covered with what covered it, his eye turned not aside, nor did it wander, for he saw the greatest of the signs of his Lord.

The details of the night journey from Mecca to Jerusalem are elaborated by various transmitters of early tradition, the versions varying from each other in some minor points. The following is a typical narration of this journey as given by Ibn Hisham in his *Life of Mohammed*[3] in the name of Al-Hasan:

The prophet of God said: While I was sleeping in the valley, came to me Gabriel and kicked me with his foot, so I sat up, but, not seeing anything, I lay again on my bed. He kicked me then once more, and I sat up and did not see a thing, so I lay back on my bed. He then kicked me a third time and I sat up; whereupon he took me by the arm, and I rose and we went to the door of the temple. There was standing a white beast,[4] between a mule and an ass (in size), with two wings on its thighs, digging in its hind legs and placing its forelegs as far as it can see. Gabriel carried me onto the beast, and we went together at the same speed.

Al-Hasan continues the story:

So the prophet of God journeyed, and with him also Gabriel, until they reached the temple in Jerusalem.[5] He found there Abraham, Moses, and Jesus, among other prophets, and he led them in prayers. Then he was given two vessels, one filled with wine and the other with milk, so the prophet of God took the vessel with milk and drank it, leaving the vessel of wine. Seeing that, Gabriel said to him: "You were guided to the true religion (*Islam*), and so was your nation, for

[2] This tree, *al-Sidra*, stands, according to the commentators, in the seventh heaven on the right side of the throne of God and nobody, not even the angels, can pass beyond it.

[3] Ed. Wüstenfeld, 364 f.

[4] Generally called *Al-Burak*, used by other prophets for their journeys, according to the tradition.

[5] In the Koran: Al-Masjid al-Aksa, the farther temple.

wine is forbidden unto you." Then the prophet of God departed to Mecca.[6]

The tradition of Mohammed's ascension to heaven is connected by many old authorities with the preceding occurrence by omitting the last sentence and continuing the story, which is given in different versions with some elaborations. It is interesting to note here that in Bokhari's *Collection of Traditions* (*Hadith*) Mohammed's ascension to heaven seems to be not connected directly with his journey to Jerusalem, the latter being referred to briefly as follows:

Jabir Ibn Abdullah heard the prophet of God saying "When the tribe of Kuraish declared me untruthful (with regard to the night journey), I stood up in the valley, and God revealed to me the temple of Jerusalem and I described it to them, while I was looking at it."[7]

Since the story of the ascension as given by Ibn Hisham[8] is greatly embellished and elaborated, Bokhari's version will be briefly presented here.

Anas b. Malik in the name of Malik b. Sa'sa'a said that the prophet of God told them of the night in which he was translated, saying: "While I was lying (sleeping) within the wall of the Caaba, Gabriel came and opened my chest and took out my heart. Then a golden basin, filled with Faith, was brought, and my heart was washed in it and stuffed with it, then it was returned to its place. Now I was given a white beast, smaller than a mule but larger than an ass [it is the Burak who makes his steps as far as his eye can see], and I was carried upon it. So Gabriel departed with me until we came to the lower heaven and asked to open it. But he was asked: 'Who are you?' — 'Gabriel.' 'Who is with you?' — 'Mohammed.' 'Was he sent for?' — 'Yes, he was.' 'Then, welcome to him,' — and it was opened. When

[6] Jalal al-Din in his Commentary on the Koran adds that when Mohammed arrived at the temple in Jerusalem, he tied Al-Burak with a rope, previously used by the prophets.

[7] Bukhari, *Kitab Bad' al-Khalk*, *bab al-Isra*, and *Kitab Tafsir al-Kor'an*, Sura "Bani Isra'il."

[8] *Life of Mohammed*, 268 ff.

I came in, I saw Adam, and Gabriel told me: 'This is your father Adam! Greet him!' So we exchanged greetings, and Adam said: 'Welcome, righteous son and righteous prophet!' After that we went up to the second heaven, and Gabriel asked to open it [the same questions and answers follow]. When I came in, I saw John and Jesus, and we exchanged greetings, and they added: 'Welcome, righteous brother and righteous prophet!' We went up then to the third heaven, and Gabriel asked to open it, etc., etc. When I came in, I saw Joseph, and we exchanged greetings, etc. Then we went up to the fourth heaven, and Gabriel asked to open it, etc., etc. When I came in, I saw Idris (Enoch), and we exchanged greetings, etc. Then we went up to the fifth heaven, and Gabriel asked to open it, etc., etc. When I came in, I saw Aaron, and we exchanged greetings, etc. Then we went up to the sixth heaven, and Gabriel asked to open it, etc., etc. When I came in, I saw Moses, and we exchanged greetings, and he said: 'Welcome, righteous brother and righteous prophet!' As I passed him by, he wept, and when asked why he weeps, he said: 'I weep because he was sent after me as prophet while a youth, and the number of those who will enter paradise will be greater of his people than of mine.' Then we went up to the seventh heaven, and Gabriel asked to open it, etc., etc. When I came in, I saw Abraham, and we exchanged greetings, and he said: 'Welcome, righteous son and righteous prophet!' Then was raised before me the *Sidra* (lote-tree) beyond which there is no passing, whose fruit is as large as the jars of Hajar (a city in Yemen) and its leaves are like the ears of an elephant. So Gabriel said: 'This is the Sidra beyond which there is no passing.' And four rivers come from its roots, two inside and two outside. So I asked Gabriel: 'What are they, O Gabriel?' And he answered: 'The two inside rivers flow in the Paradise, and the outside two are the Nile and the Euphrates.' Then was raised before me the Inhabited House, in which seventy thousand angels enter every day. Later I was given a vessel of wine, a vessel of milk, and a vessel of honey; so I took the milk, and Gabriel said: 'You and your people have the true religion.' I was commanded then to pray fifty prayers every day. On my return I passed by Moses, and he asked me: 'What were you commanded?' — 'Fifty prayers every day.' 'Your people will surely not be able to pray fifty prayers each day. By God, I had experience with people before you, and I had the greatest contention with the children of Israel, so better go back and ask the Lord to make it easier for your people.' So I went back (to the Lord) and He took off ten prayers. Returning to Moses, he said to me the same as before, so I went back (to the Lord), and He took off another ten prayers, etc. Then I was commanded to pray five prayers each day. Returning to Moses, he said to me again the same as before, but I told him that I asked the Lord so much that I feel ashamed, I shall therefore be satisfied and obey [become a Moslem]. As I passed by, the crier called me, and I executed the command and made it easier for my worshippers."[9]

Another version is quoted by some authorities that Mohammed made his night journey not while he was drowsing within the enclosure of the Caaba, but during some night that he spent in the house of Umm Hani', the daughter of Abu Talib. According to Ibn Hisham she emphatically stated:

The prophet of God made his night journey only during the night that he slept in my house. He prayed the last evening prayer, then we all went to sleep. Towards day-break the prophet of God woke us up and after praying the morning prayer together he said: 'O Umm Hani', I prayed with you here the last evening prayer, as you witnessed it, then I went to the temple in Jerusalem and prayed there, and now I have prayed with you the morning prayer, as you see.' He then got up to go out, but I got hold of the end of his cloak and said unto him: 'O prophet of God, do not tell this to people, for they will think that you are lying, and they will cause you injury.' So he said: 'By God, I shall tell them about it!' Then I said to my Abyssinian slave-girl: 'Woe unto you! Follow the prophet of God and hear what he will say to the people and what they will say to him.'[10]

When the people to whom he told of his journey doubted its veracity, he described to them and, according to some authorities, to Abu Bekr not only the temple in Jerusalem, but even the herds of camels, belonging to various tribes, which he saw during his journey to Palestine, and they all had to admit that he told the truth.

While most of the theologians fully believe that Mohammed

[9] Bukhari, *Kitab Bad' al-Khalk, bab al-Mi'raj*. The story as related in *Kitab al-Sala* is somewhat different.

[10] Ibn Hisham, *Life of Mohammed*, 267.

actually made his night journey to Jerusalem and ascended to heaven in body, there is the opinion of some of the oldest authorities,[11] such as Al-Hasan b. Abi Al-Hasan, Mu'awiya b. Abi Sufyan, and A'isha, the prophet's wife, that both events took place in a dream, that it was a vision of his spirit, not an actual experience of his body. They find support for their opinion in the following verse of the Koran (XVII, 62): "We have appointed the vision which we showed thee . . . only for an occasion of dispute unto men," the expression *Ru'ya*, vision, usually referring to something seen in a dream, though also to day-dreaming while fully awake. The introductory words of Mohammed in relating his story: "While I was sleeping," "While I was neither asleep, nor awake," tend to strengthen their opinion that it was a dream. There is even a tradition reported in the name of A'isha, which expressly states, that "the prophet of God never was missed in his body, but he made his night journey in his spirit."[12] However, the preponderant majority of Moslem authorities is inclined to take both events in a literal sense, that in either case the story refers to an actual experience, and not to a vision. They accept them as great miracles, notwithstanding several passages in the Koran, where the fact is emphasized that Mohammed was sent only as warner and preacher, as for example, "And they who believe not say: 'If a sign from his Lord be not sent down to him . . .!' Thou art a warner only. And every people hath its guide"[13] (Sura XIII, 8).

It is interesting to note here the opinion of a modern Moslem authority, Maulvi Muhammed Ali, President, Ahmadiah Anjaman-I-Ishaet-I-Islam, Lahore, India. In his English trans-

[11] Ibn Hisham, 265; Zamakhshari's commentary on Sura XVII, 1.

[12] *Ibid.* Zamakhshari, *loc. cit.*, has ". . . but he was taken to heaven in his spirit."

[13] See also Koran XIII, 27; XVII, 95; XXV, 8 ff.; XXIX, 44.

lation and commentary, published in England in 1917, he makes the following comment on Sura XVII, 1:

This journey is generally supposed to refer to the ascension (Mi'raj) of the Holy Prophet. . . If the reference here is to the mi'raj, the significance underlying it is the future triumph of the cause of the Holy Prophet. But the reference may as well be to the Holy Prophet's coming Flight to Medina. It was at night that the Holy Prophet left Mecca (Ibn-i-Hisham). The remote mosque would in this case mean the Prophet's mosque which was to be built at Medina, or Medina itself, as the Sacred Mosque stands for Mecca. Or it may signify Jerusalem, the significance being that the Prophet shall inherit all the blessings of the Israelite prophets, including the Holy Land. (p. 561, n. 1410)

The nature of Mohammed's ascension to heaven is explained by him in the following comment on verse 60 (62) of this Sura:

"Most commentators agree that the reference here is to the vision of Ascension (Bkh, Rz), which gave the Holy Prophet promises of great success after his flight, because so the vision of Ascension to heaven is to be interpreted. There has been a difference of opinion among the learned as to whether the Holy Prophet's ascension was bodily or spiritual; the majority adhere to the first view, but among those who hold the latter view there are personages of sound opinion, such as 'Ayeshah and Mu'aviah. In view of the plain words of the Qur-an, however, which refer to the ascension as being the vision which We showed you, the opinion of the majority must be rejected. The Qur-an on several occasions mentions even visions without describing them as visions. But when it is plainly called a vision, not the least reason exists to question its nature. The sayings of the Holy Prophet do not indeed say whether it was a vision or not, but the circumstances related clearly show it to be a vision. Thus in a report received through Sharik, it is stated that the angel came to him: 'On another night when his heart saw (things) and his eyes slept but his heart did not sleep'; and the concluding words of this report are: 'And he awoke and he was in the Sacred Mosque' (Bukhari, *Kitab ul Tauhid*). In another report the words describing the condition in which he was at the time of ascension are: 'Whilst I was in a state between that of one sleeping and one awake.' In fact, it is quite true that he was not asleep; he was in a vision though not in a dream, but at the same time it was not a corporeal ascension. He was actually carried to the Holy Presence, and he was shown great wonders, but it was in spirit that he was carried, and it was with the spiritual eye that he saw those wonders, not in body and with the physical eye, for things spiritual can only be seen with the spiritual eye. And this vision had an important significance. He saw it at a time when his condition was, to human seeming, one of utmost helplessness, and he was shown that a great future lay before him. His opponents, as usual, disbelieved in such visions, and laughed at them" (p. 578, n. 1441).

With regard to the time when the night journey took place, the most accepted opinion is that it occurred about a year before the Hijra. Yet there is the opinion of Anas and Al-Hasan that it took place before Mohammed was sent as prophet, while others think that it happened five years later.[14]

[14] Zamakhshari; Baidawi; Kastalani on Bukhari, *loc. cit.*

The Prohibition of Wine in the Mohammedan Religion

WHILE the subject of my present paper has nothing to do directly with anything Jewish, I feel it may not be without interest to the members of *Dorshe Da'at*. For whatever has to do with *Mashkeh* (liquor) is of particular interest to the Jew, because *machen le-chayim* (drinking a toast) became almost an institution with the Orthodox Jew. In the old Orthodox synagogue a little *Mashkeh* regularly followed the morning or evening prayer at every *yorzeit*. As for the Ḥasid, the same *Mashkeh* frequently was the source of the exalted state of mind prerequisite for devotional service; some aspiring candidate for a Ph. D. may yet take the subject of "The Effect of Prohibition on Ḥasidism" as a theme for his dissertation. But this is not the subject of the present study, which is on the prohibition of wine among our cousins, the Arabs.

The general prohibition of wine drinking in the Moslem religion is based essentially on two verses in the Koran which read as follows: "They will ask thee concerning wine and games of chance. Say: In both is great sin, and advantage also, to men; but their sin is greater than their advantage" (Sura II, 216). "O believers! Surely wine, and games of chance, and statues, and divining arrows, are an abomination of Satan's work; therefore avoid them, that ye may prosper" (Sura V, 92).

The question whether this prohibition is limited to grapewine only, or also includes all other intoxicating drinks, was the subject of a great deal of controversy among the early Moslem authorities. Omar, one of the Companions of the Prophet, is reported to have delivered a sermon that "the wine prohibited in the Koran embraces five kinds: of grapes, of dates, of honey, of wheat, and of barley. Wine is that which obscures the understanding" (Bukhari's *Collection of Islamic Traditions, Book on Drinks*, 2 and 5). Another tradition was reported by A'isha, Mohammed's favorite wife, that the Prophet of Allah was asked about *nabidh* made of honey, much used by the people of Yemen, and he said that any drink which intoxicates is forbidden. This strict interpretation was followed by the conservative theologians, who proscribed the use of any strong drink in addition to the traditional grapewine. The controversy was especially bitter over *nabidh*, an intoxicating drink made of green or ripe dates, much used by the Arabs, but banned by the orthodox Moslems.

Their line of argument was that "the real reason why grapewine was prohibited is that it causes drunkenness, dissension, and forsaking God and His prayers. Now, these same reasons could be well applied also to *nabidh*, and therefore it should be treated exactly the same as grapewine. This case is the same, they argued, as the *Hadith* of the Prophet, may Allah pray for him and give him peace, about a mouse that fell into melted butter; if the mouse be dead, then it is thrown out and the butter around it is discarded too; but if the mouse be alive, then all of the butter has to be thrown out. Now this regulation has been correctly applied by the theologians also to olive oil and the like, for it is evident that the Prophet of Allah did not really mean here butter in particular that was contaminated by a mouse, but it just happened that he was asked about melted butter, and he rendered his decision; and it could also be applied to olive oil and other fats as well. Similar is the case with the prohibition of drinking grapewine: it should be applied to *nabidh* too, since it has the same intoxicating qualities."[1]

The liberal theologians, on the other hand, clung to the

[1] *Al-'Iḳd al-Farid*, IV, Cairo, 1913, p. 332.

literal interpretation of this interdiction — namely, that only *khamr*, grapewine, is forbidden — and considered all other fermented drinks, including *nabidh*, as lawfully permitted, the term *khamr* not being applicable to them. Furthermore, they even claimed that "the reason why Allah forbade the use of grapewine is not in order to avoid drunkenness, nor because it is an abomination, but merely as a devotional measure; otherwise, Allah would surely not have permitted its use to the early prophets, nor to the nations of the past. Neither would Noah have drunk wine after he had left the Ark, nor Jesus at the Last Supper, nor the Companions of Mohammed at the inception of Islam. The term "abomination" that is applied to wine should also be taken not in its literal sense, for it certainly is not filthy nor ill smelling. What it really means is that grapewine is prohibited as if it were an abomination, just as in the case of adultery, to which this term is likewise applied."[2]

Between these two extreme views, the strictly orthodox and the liberal, there is the moderate opinion presented by Ibn Kutaiba in his *Book on Drinks*. He maintains that "Allah has forbidden grapewine in the Koran and intoxicants in His oral tradition. The former, therefore, is prohibited unconditionally in any quantity whatever, whereas the use of intoxicants is forbidden only in quantities that would intoxicate, but their moderate use should be permitted. If, for example, a man gets intoxicated when he drinks four glasses of *nabidh*, it is only the fourth glass that really caused his intoxication, and this he is prohibited to drink, but the first three could not in his case be considered as intoxicants at all, and he should be permitted to drink them. It is similar to the case of four men assailing a fifth man in a drunken fight. The first one gave the victim a blow and tore the skin of his head; the second fractured his skull with another blow; the third assailant knocked him to the

[2] *Op. cit.*, p. 334.

ground, and the fourth finished the victim by hitting him on the brain. It is evident that the responsibility for this murder could be laid to the fourth assailant only, and not to the first three, from whose blows the victim could probably have recovered."[3]

Other authorities, of a more radical trend of mind, quoted the following verse from the Koran: "And of the fruit of the palmtrees, and of the grapes, ye obtain an inebriating drink, and also good nourishment. Verily herein is a sign unto people who understand" (Sura XVI, 69), which they interpreted as permission to use even grapewine in moderation. However, according to the standard commentaries, Jalalein, Al-Zamakhshari, and Al-Baidawi, this verse was revealed before the drinking of wine was prohibited.

In connection with the last-mentioned verse, an interesting story is related by Al-Zamakhshari in his commentary on the Koran, which may have some bearing as to the cause of the rise and development of this interdiction. On account of its importance it may be of interest to quote it here in full.

"Four verses were revealed in reference to wine. It was revealed in Mecca, 'And of the fruits of palm-trees, and of grapes, ye obtain an inebriating drink' (Sura XVI, 69), so the Moslems drank wine freely, since it was permitted to them. Thereupon Omar, Maad, and Nafr, of the Companions of Mohammed, said: 'O Prophet of God, give us a legal decision with respect to *khamr* (wine), for it verily removeth understanding and despoileth wealth.' Then the following revelation came down: 'In both (wine and games of chance) is a great sin, and advantage also, to men' (Sura II, 216), with the result that some people still indulged in drinking wine, while others abstained from it. After that, Abd al-Rahman ibn Awf invited some people to a banquet, and they drank and became intoxicated. Then one of them rose to lead in the prayers and

[3] *Op. cit.*, p. 330–1.

recited: 'Say! O ye unbelievers! I worship not that which ye worship' (Sura CIX, 1–2), whereupon this verse was revealed: 'Come not near prayer when ye are drunk, but wait till ye can understand what ye say' (Sura IV, 46); so the number of those who drank grew less. Later Otban ibn Malik invited some friends to his house, among them also Saad ibn Abi Wakkas. After they became drunk, they began to boast and recite verses to each other, and Saad recited a verse wherein there was a slur on the Ansar (Helpers of Mohammed). An Ansari who was present thereat struck him with a jaw-bone of a camel and fractured his skull, then went to complain to the Prophet of God, may God pray for him and give him peace. Thereupon Omar said: 'By Allah! Give us an unequivocal explanation in the question of wine'; so forthwith came down the following revelation: 'O believers! Surely wine, and games of chance, and statues, and divining arrows, are an abomination of Satan's work; therefore avoid them, that ye may prosper. Satan seeketh to sow dissension and hatred among you, by means of wine and games of chance, and to turn you aside from the remembrance of God, and from prayer: will ye not, therefore, abstain from them?' (Sura V, 92–93). Then Omar, may God be gracious to him, said: 'We abstain, O Lord!' "

We probably have in this report the conditions which brought about the gradual development of this prohibition. It seems that at first even the Prophet himself looked rather favorably on the fruit of the grape, comparing its beneficial effects to that of the fruit of the palm-tree. It was only at the insistence of the very pious Omar and two other companions of the Prophet that a half-hearted admission of the sinfulness of drinking wine was pronounced, with an exonerative clause, however, that it does render some benefit to men. When a true believer, wishing to lead in prayer, rose and, under the influence of drink, recited the wrong passage in the Koran, addressing his fellow-believers:

"Say: O ye unbelievers," etc., a law was enacted not to come to prayers, when one is intoxicated.[4] This naturally implies, if not a full permission, at least a toleration of a state of intoxication during the hours between prayers. But the question soon reached its crucial point when the most important political group, the Ansar, the helpers of Mohammed in the holy wars, were sneered at, as a result of overindulgence and drunkenness. The offender was severely punished, and a complaint was brought to the Prophet. He now saw that the time had arrived for decisive action: strife and dissension were developing among his immediate helpers because of excessive use of the fruit of the vine. Omar pressed the issue to its logical conclusion, emphatically demanding a peremptory decision, not a half-way measure similar to the one enacted previously with regard to prayer. The consequence was a drastic prohibition of the use of wine, or, as some authorities say, of all inebriating drinks, at all times, stamping it as "an abomination of Satan's work."

That the Arabs were far from being a temperate people is shown by the fact that wine and drink occupy an important place in their classical poetry. Some Arabs were so addicted to drink that in spite of imprisonment and various other punishments they could not keep away from it and openly violated the law of prohibition. So Abu Mihjan al-Thakafi, a well known poet who flourished during the reign of the Khalif Omar I in the first century of the Hijra, wrote: "Give me, oh friend, wine to drink, though well I know what God has revealed with respect to wine. Serve me pure wine, and let my sin be greater, for only when one drinks it unmixed does the sin become complete." And notwithstanding the punishment that he suffered at the hand of the pious Khalif Omar, his last wish was: "When I die, bury me at the root of a vine, so that my bones may become

[4] Compare with this the biblical prohibition of wine and strong drink for priests, when they entered the Tabernacle (Lev. 10. 9), and for Nazirites (Num. 6. 3).

saturated with its juice. Do not bury me in a plain, for fear that I shall then never get the taste of wine when dead." [5]

A similar thought was expressed by another "Bohemian" poet of the Umayyad period: "Once dead, let a vine my shroud be, and use my grave as cellar for wine." Abu Nuwas (died about 810 C. E.), one of the most celebrated poets in Arabic literature, is especially known for his wine-songs, which are remarkable for their beauty and frankness. Here is R. A. Nicholson's rendition of one of his shorter poems: [6] —

> Thou scolder of the grape and me,
> I ne'er shall win thy smile!
> Because against thee I rebel,
> 'Tis churlish to revile.
>
> Ah, breathe no more the name of wine
> Until thou cease to blame,
> For fear that thy foul tongue should smirch
> Its fair and lovely name!
>
> Come, pour it out, ye gentle boys,
> A vintage ten years old,
> That seems as though 'twere in the cup
> A lake of liquid gold.
>
> And when the water mingles there,
> To fancy's eye are set
> Pearls over shining pearls close strung
> As in a carcanet.

Abu Nuwas was the boon-companion and genial friend of the celebrated Caliph Harun al-Rashid, of *Arabian Nights*' fame, who likewise was far from temperate. The fact is that many of the caliphs, who were religious monarchs and bore the title "Commander of the Faithful," frequently indulged in drunkenness and intemperance, thus openly violating a religious law which was rather difficult to enforce.

[5] (*Kitāb al-Aġāni*, XXI, p. 140).

[6] *Literary History of the Arabs*, New York, 1907, p. 294. The Arabic original was edited by Ahlwardt, *Diwan des Abu Nowas . . . Die Weinlieder*, No. 47.

We have indications that even Mohammed himself appreciated the delights of wine. In the revelation concerning it, the paradise promised to the true believer is depicted in the following terms: "A picture of the Paradise which is promised to the God-fearing: therein are rivers of water, which corrupt not; rivers of milk, whose taste changeth not; and rivers of wine, delicious to those who drink it" (Sura XLVII, 16). Thus we see that while wine is forbidden to the Moslem in this world, its free use is promised to him in the world to come. However, the wine of Paradise will be void of its intoxicating qualities, and will therefore be freely used without any ill effects.

In this connection it is interesting to quote the retribution that a Moslem, habitually addicted to drink, is going to suffer in his future existence, according to the tradition of the Prophet (*Hadith*). In the *Book on Drinks* of Bukhari's *Collection of Islamic Traditions*, we find this tradition reported in the name of Abdullah ibn Omar: "The Prophet of God, may God pray for him and give him peace, said: 'Whoever indulged in drinking wine in this world and never repented from it (i. e. never gave it up), will be forbidden to drink it in the world to come.' " Of especial interest is Kastelani's comment on this, namely: "It is quite evident that it means that the one who is addicted to drink will be refused admission to Paradise, for wine is the drink of its inhabitants, and as this sinner will be forbidden to drink it, he will necessarily fall victim to sadness and anxiety, and there can be neither sadness nor anxiety in the Paradise. . . It really means: his punishment will be that he will be forbidden to drink wine in the world to come as result of his exclusion from Paradise." Distinction is also made between the one who drinks wine, being ignorant of the law that its use is prohibited, and the one who does it willfully, being fully aware of its interdiction. The latter will never be able to drink wine in his after-life, for he will be forever excluded from Paradise, while the former may be pardoned by Allah, according to His will.

Moslem Pilgrimage to the Holy Cities

THE DUTY of every Moslem to make a pilgrimage to Mecca at least once in his life is essentially based on the following verses in the Koran III, 90–92:

Verily the first house appointed unto men to worship in was that which was in Becca;[1] blessed, and a direction to all creatures. Therein are manifest signs: the place where Abraham stood; and whoever entereth therein, shall be safe. And it is a duty towards God, incumbent on those who are able to go thither, to visit this house; but whosoever disbelieveth, verily God needeth not the service of any creature.

The "manifest signs," referred to here, are, according to the standard commentators, the sacred stone where the imprints of Abraham's feet are shown; the inviolable security of the place, mentioned here; that birds do not alight on the roof of the Caaba and wild beasts hold off from attacking their prey there, and that no hostile expedition against it ever succeeded. These commentators similarly report that Mohammed was asked: "Which is the first temple that was founded for mankind?" And his answer was: "The Temple in Mecca, and next to it is the Temple in Jerusalem, the period between them being forty years."

More explicit instructions in regard to the pilgrimage are given in Sura II, 192:

Accomplish the pilgrimage of Mecca, and the visitation[2] of God; and if ye be besieged, send that offering which shall be easiest; . . . When

[1] Becca is another name for Mecca.

[2] The "Visitation" is a minor pilgrimage which can be performed at any time except the season of the greater Pilgrimage.

ye are secure from enemies, he who contents himself with the visitation of the Temple of Mecca until the pilgrimage shall bring the offering which shall be the easiest.

Verse 193:

The pilgrimage must be performed in the known months:[3] whosoever therefore purposeth to go on pilgrimage therein, let him not know a woman, nor transgress, nor quarrel on the pilgrimage.

The more important ceremonies to be performed in connection with the pilgrimage are: "A visit to the Temple; compassing the Caaba seven times; running between the Mounts Safa and Merwa in the valley of Mina, also seven times; rushing to Mount Arafat for prayer and devotion, then returning to Mina; seven stones to be thrown at three pillars to drive the devil away; after which the sacrifices are to be slaughtered, the pilgrims and their friends eating part, and the rest being given to the poor. This over, the pilgrims shave their heads and cut their nails. This completes the pilgrimage, though the Caaba is usually revisited to take leave of the Temple. No visit to any other city is included in, or can take the place of this pilgrimage to Mecca, as stipulated in the Koran and in the authentic tradition, not even Medina, which was considered very sacred by Mohammed, a whole section being devoted in Bukhari's *Hadith* to expound its greatness.

During the great controversy between the followers of Ali and those of Othman, however, the Omayyad Caliph Abd-al-Malik (685–705 C. E.) became quite apprehensive lest his rival Abdullah Ibn Zubair, ruler of Mecca, persuade or force the pilgrims from Syria to join his ranks, and he therefore forbade the pilgrimage to Mecca. When the people protested, referring to the ordinance of the Prophet, he proposed that they make the pilgrimage to Jerusalem instead, claiming that going around

[3] These months are Shawal, Dhu-l-Kaada, and Dhu-l-Hajja.

the holy places in this city has the same power as that of the Caaba, required in Mohammedan law.[4] In order to give more sanctification and greater magnificence to Jerusalem as a place of pilgrimage, he caused to erect a cupola structure, the *Kubbat al-Sakhra*, on the place where, according to tradition, Mohammed alighted after his famous night journey. He then gave out an ordinance that the *Kubbat al-Sakhra* was just as sacred a place for *Hajj* (pilgrimage) as the Caaba in Mecca.

In this religious reform Abd-al-Malik needed, of course, the approval of authoritative theologians who would find (or compose) the necessary tradition (*Hadith*) to meet his purpose. This task was undertaken by the pious theologian Al-Zuhri who invented and widely spread an alleged tradition of the Prophet to the effect that "there are three mosques to which pilgrimage may be made: in Mecca, in Medina, and in Jerusalem."[5] The obvious tendency of this *Hadith* is shown by the addition of the following sentence, often omitted by later theologians: "And a prayer in the *Beit al-Makdis* in Jerusalem is better than a thousand prayers in any other sanctuary,"[6] thus including also that of Mecca or Medina. The story that every year in the night of Arafat the Zemzem well in Mecca makes a visit to the well of Siloah in Jerusalem is intended to show that the latter city likewise has a well equally wondrous as the Zemzem in Mecca.[7] A woman of the entourage of Mohammed by the name of Maimuna is supposed to have asked him: "Give us a decision with respect to *Beit al-Makdis* (the Temple in Jerusalem)!" Whereupon he answered: "Make a pilgrimage to this temple and pray therein — war was then prevalent in the

[4] Goldziher, *Muhammedanische Studien*, II, pp. 35 f.

[5] Al-Ya'kubi, II, p. 311.

[6] Ibn al-Fakih al-Hammadani, p. 95, 3.

[7] Yakut, III, p. 726, 7.

land — and if it be impossible for you to go there, send oil for its lamps."[8]

It may be stated here in passing that Al-Zuhri circulated these *Hadiths* not for selfish reasons, but for consideration of the state, for the unselfishness of this theologian is highly praised by his contemporary Amr ben Dinar.[9] Such traditions became wide-spread even in later times, when the pilgrimage to Jerusalem was considered as equally important as the one to Mecca, referring to Abd al-Malik as authority. In fact, the Syrians were untiring in circulating *Hadiths* which accentuate the superiority of their sanctuaries, making them of equal importance with the holy places of Hijaz.[10]

[8] Abu Dawud, I, p. 46. These quotations are given by Goldziher, *op. cit.*, pp. 36 f.

[9] *Ibid.*, p. 38.

[10] *Ibid.*, p. 36.

Bee-Keeping in the Holy Land in the Time of Jesus

HONEY and bees were known in the Holy Land — the land that flows with milk and honey — from days immemorial. The Bible refers to bees on numerous occasions. Wild bees were found in the clefts of the rocks and in the hollow of trees, as witness Psalms (81:17), "And with honey out of the rock would I satisfy thee," and in I Samuel (14:25), "And all they of the land came to a wood, and there was honey upon the ground, "etc.

Wild bees are also referred to in Judges (14:89), "When Samson turned to see the carcass of the lion; and behold, there was a swarm of bees and honey in the carcass of the lion. And he took thereof in his hands and went on eating and came to his father and mother and he gave them and they did eat." A swarm of wild bees is compared to a hostile army attacking the nation, and the picture depicted in the Psalms (118:12), "They compassed me like bees" is quite familiar to every bee-keeper.

Honey became a staple article of diet with the ancient Hebrews, and is spoken of in the Bible in conjunction with corn, oil, wine, and "all the increase in the field." "Hast thou found honey?" we read in the Proverbs (25:16), "eat so much as is sufficient for thee, lest thou be filled therewith, and vomit it." It was so abundant in the Holy Land that it was even exported to foreign markets (Ezekiel 27:17). A vegetable honey was also prepared by boiling down the juice of dates into a syrup, and was used quite extensively in Palestine.

There is a legend current about King Solomon that when the

Queen of Sheba visited him, she wished to test his reputed great wisdom, and brought to his presence two wreaths of flowers. One was made up of the choicest live flowers in her garden, the other was an exact copy of the former, but executed by very skilful hands. The wise king was requested to tell at sight which wreath was of genuine flowers.

The great king became somewhat embarrassed at this difficult task, much to the surprise of his numerous admirers, as well as the fair inquirer, the Queen of Sheba. Suddenly he noticed a number of bees clustering to the window in front of him. He immediately ordered to open the window, and all the bees rushed straight to the wreath of the live flowers. "Here is the wreath!" rejoiced King Solomon to the amazed Queen, and all present admired his great wisdom forever more.

Subsequently, in the beginning of the Christian era, we find bee-keeping a pretty well developed industry in the Holy Land. In the Talmud, that great encyclopaedia of Hebrew thought, we find a great deal of information scattered here and there on the state of agriculture in the early centuries of our era.

There were several types of hives in use at that time. The old straw scap was ever present, while some were of wicker work. One type of hive was constructed in the shape of a wooden barrel lying on its side. Its bottom could be opened to enable the taking out of the honey, while the top board was made full of small holes serving as exits for the bees. Some of these holes were at times packed with straw in order to lessen, if necesssry, the number of exits.

When combs full with honey were ready to be taken out, the bees were first stupefied by smoke. And it is interesting to note that a special vessel was used for that purpose, where dried cow manure was burned, and the smoke thus produced pacified the bees while taking off the honey, just as we are doing now with our modern smokers. The name of this vessel, *middoph*, which indicates in Hebrew "blowing," shows that it had some contrivance to form an air current, and thus keep the fire going. — So here we possess indications of a smoker in use in the Holy Land some eighteen hundred years before it ever became known to us!

A number of interesting legal provisions pertaining to bee-keeping in the first centuries of our era are found in the Talmud. In case one sells the natural increase of his hive, he is supposed to deliver to the buyer the first swarm and two afterswarms. Some habits of bees are described in this connection. They have a tendency to swarm in the beginning of summer; a primary swarm issues from the hive, then, some nine days later, an afterswarm follows it, which is considered much inferior to the first one. It is also pointed out that in Greece a colony sometimes sends out seven or eight swarms, one following the other. Feeding bees mustard is advised as a means to curtail their swarming tendency.

Another legal provision is brought out in case a bee-keeper sells in advance the combs with honey of his hive. The buyer is entitled then at the end of the season to all the combs with honey found in the hive but two, which are to be left in the hive for the bees for wintering. The explanation following in connection with this provision is also interesting. After the swarms have issued from the hive, the remaining bees settle to gather honey. They store the honey in some ten or twenty combs, and whoever sells only the combs, and not his colony of bees, intends to preserve the latter for next year. He is, therefore, entitled to two combs at least as food for his bees during winter. There is here more consideration for bees than that of many a modern bee-keeper who often extracts so closely that there is hardly anything left for his bees to winter on.

There are also provisions against adulteration of honey by admixture of water or flour. So here we have some pure food regulations many centuries before our Congress passed in 1906 the national pure food bill. Honey by itself was considered a beverage, and its uses were manifold. A drink compounded of honey, oil, and wine is mentioned in the Talmud. It was also used as medicine in numerous cases, as well as in embalming.

We can thus have a pretty fair idea about the comparatively high development of bee-keeping in the Holy Land in the time of Jesus. The fact that special legislation had to be enacted to regulate the industry proves that it had been quite extensive, and played an important role in the industrial life of the country.

Swarming

A Study in Bee Behavior

THE STUDY of the behavior of bees under the swarming impulse is both interesting and important to every progressive bee-keeper. Its importance is best illustrated by the late Dr. C. C. Miller's statement (*Fifty Years among the Bees*, p. 151), "If I were to meet a man perfect in the entire science and art of beekeeping, and were allowed from him an answer to just one question, I would ask for the best and easiest way to prevent swarming, for one who is anxious to secure the largest crop of comb honey."

Swarming has been carefully studied by various investigators as well as by many practical bee-keepers for several years. Different theories have been advanced as to its fundamental causes, yet this question is far from being settled. Lack of sufficient ventilation during hot weather, the queen being crowded for space, peculiar conditions of certain localities and seasons are, after all, only contributory causes, which, important as they are in augmenting and promoting the swarming fever, could hardly be considered more than conditions favoring the tendency of swarming.

The Russian bee-keepers hold, as a general cause of swarming, the natural tendency of bees, as of many other insects of their class, to form new colonies in that way. Just as the old worn-out bees are being constantly supplanted under favorable conditions by young bees emerging from the cells, so are the old families headed by old queens being supplanted by new families and young queens taking the place of their mothers. It is just the natural law of reproduction and of propagation of the species applied to whole colonies, a kind of community reproduction in the same sense as individual reproduction. To quote Frank C. Pellett (*Productive Beekeeping*, p. 100), "It should be remembered that with bees and other social insects the community is the unit, rather than the individual. The workers are incapable of reproduction, and accordingly no matter how great an increase there may be in their number in the hive, it is but temporary, and makes no permanent difference in the perpetuation of the species. Swarming is then the expression of the instinct of procreation or increase."

Of course, one can frequently observe in the same apiary a large percentage of colonies that pass through the entire season without making any attempt to swarm at all. But then the procreative instinct is not developed with all communities, as with all individuals, alike. Besides, there are many special causes which diminish and control the swarming tendency among the bees, as old crippled bees, weak colonies, young queens, etc.

According to the opinion of the German investigator, Gerstung (quoted by Dr. Phillips, *Beekeeping*, 1915, p. 79), swarming is caused by undue proportion of nurse bees to the young brood they have to feed with larval food, or royal jelly. The hive is full of capped brood before swarming, but very little of young larvae or eggs are found there at that time. The presence of an excessive quantity of larval food induces the bees to build queen cells and rear queens by the surplus food. W. Z. Hutchinson (*Advanced Bee Culture*, 5th edition, p. 64) and E. R. Root (*A. B. C. and X. Y. Z. of Bee Culture*, 1920, article "Swarming") are inclined to accept this theory as the prime cause of swarming.

While this preponderance of nurse bees in the brood chamber is a general condition in all colonies shortly before swarming, it could hardly be considered more than one of its chief notable symptoms, on the same order as the invariable procedure of a swarming colony to construct drone comb, depositing drone eggs, and building queen cells. All these symptoms will be manifested in various regions and in different seasons in accordance with the special conditions of the honey flow, favoring the rapid increase of the population of the hive, which in its turn tends to develop the procreative instinct of the community as a whole. The fact that a colony could be induced to give up swarming by taking away all young brood and substituting for them empty combs would indicate that excess of larval food is not the prime cause of swarming, since in this case the food would immediately be increased instead of being diminished (Demuth, quoted in above-mentioned article on "Swarming").

So far the question of the fundamental cause of swarming is far from being definitely solved. Unfortunately, too little attention has been paid by serious investigators to this important phase of bee behavior. While the practical bee-keeper sought to devise various methods for controlling swarming by removing for the time being the contributory causes which tend to develop the swarming fever, he did very little to find out the prime cause of this phenomenon.

Numerous methods have been employed for the prevention of swarming. Root, in his article on swarming (*A. B. C. and X. Y. Z. of Bee Culture*, 1920) sums up 12 different methods, whereas some Russian text books quote as many as twenty methods for swarm control. However, to all of them would apply Demuth's conclusion, that "any manipulation for swarm control, whether applied after the colony has acquired the swarming fever or applied to all colonies alike previous to the swarming season, is based upon the single principle — a temporary disturbance in the continuity of the daily emergence of brood. This disturbance should occur just previous to or during the swarming season (Demuth, "Comb Honey," 1917, *Farmers' Bulletin*, 505, p. 34).

Swarming season varies greatly, according to climatic conditions of different regions, but May and June could generally be considered as swarming months, while in the South swarming begins somewhat earlier.

The procedure of swarming itself is so beautifully depicted by Langstroth, Cheshire, Maeterlink and others, that I shall give here only a brief description, with due regard to the behavior of bees during the process of swarming.

When the flow of nectar is coming in pretty regularly, brood rearing being thereby greatly stimulated, our bee community becomes very populous. The provident bees start to build drone combs and the queen deposits drone eggs therein.

Queen cells are started before the maturing of the drones in their cells. The number of queen cells are rarely less than three or more than thirty, although a bee-keeper from Palestine told me that fifty to a hundred queen cells built under the swarming impulse is a frequent occurence with their native bees. When the cells have already been capped, we may expect swarming any fair warm day.

The following table made by the Russian bee-keeper, Butkewitch (Butkewitch, *Manual of Beekeeping* (Russian), St. Petersburg, 1911), may be of some value to the practical beekeeper:

From Stages of Development of Queen Cells	*Number of Days*	
	To prime Swarm	To after Swarm
From the depositing of an egg in queen cell	10	18
From the appearance of young larva	7	15
From the sealing of the cell	2	10
Issuing of prime swarm	0	8
From the "piping" of the virgins		1

The bees do not entirely suspend their work on the day they intend to leave their hive. I have frequently observed colonies where the bees were going on with gathering nectar in the morning about the same as usual, yet they swarmed in the afternoon. Neither do the clusters hanging outside the hives invariably signify that those particular colonies are preparing to swarm. Such "hanging out" is probably in most cases due to hot weather and to lack of ventilation.

The colony is often unusually quiet before the swarm is to issue, reminding one of the quietude of the weather before the coming storm. The first signs of excitement are frequently revealed by the queen, who seems to be very restless on the day she is to leave. Instead of her regular routine of work of laying eggs, she is somewhat agitated, aimlessly running around over the combs. Soon the whole colony is in an uproar. Several bees fly and dance in the air in front of the hive with their heads toward it, as though anticipating the coming rush. Yet in the midst of their great agitation they do not forget to provide themselves with a good supply of honey to last them for a few days.

Meanwhile the commotion in the hive is growing rapidly. Young and old are literally "pouring out" of the hive, as though some mysterious force is relentlessly driving them from their old home. They rush onward as fast as they can, tending to go upward, take wing, and begin to gyrate rythmically, at first around the hive, then extending the area of their merry-making larger and larger until it occupies a large portion of the apiary. There is something elemental in the whole procedure. They seem to abandon themselves completely to their hilarious joy, ringing their wings in great excitement, with a certain rhythm in all their motions.

There is no set rule when the queen leaves the hive. The idea that she leads the swarm is erroneous, for she frequently leaves the hive when about a third or a half of the emigrants are out. She sometimes falls to the ground in her attempt to take wing together with the madly rushing bees, being heavily loaded with eggs and probably dazzled by the bright light of the sun. After a short rest in front of the hive she is up again in the air among her family.

The number of bees participating in a swarm is estimated variously. The Russian bee-keepers consider a good prime swarm at six to seven pounds, which quantity coincides with Dr. Phillips' estimate of 35,000 (*Beekeeping*, 1915, p. 39), considering about 5,000 bees to the pound.

The old idea that all kinds of noise made while the swarm is in the air would induce it to settle is disproved by modern investigators, although Cheshire thinks that there is some truth in it, and on the whole it is correct. It was also probably done in order to inform the neighbors about the issuance of a swarm and thus sustain its ownership. Langstroth reports that flashing the rays of the sun by means of a mirror would make it settle, while many old bee-keepers used to throw mud or water for the same purpose, as well as for preventing the joining of two or more swarms together.

Bees, participating in the swarm, being filled with honey are not apt to sting. Yet the general idea among the beekeepers that they *will never sting* is probably wrong, because they do sting under provocation, even while swarming.

But here our merry-makers in the air, after whirling in large circles and dancing for a while, begin to settle in a cluster not very far from their old home. The old queen, heavy with eggs, weak and not used to light and flying, cannot ordinarily make a long flight without first resting, and wherever she alights, the bees cluster with her. Frequently, she alights on a spot where some bees have been clustering previous to her arrival.

The wind seems to have a great deal to do with the direction in which a swarm flies. The apiary where I had the opportunity to study swarming had a windbreak of eucalyptus trees, the hives being situated, of course, on the side from the wind, where its force was broken by the trees. On the other side of the apiary was an alfalfa field in which direction the wind was blowing. Out of fifty cases of swarming that I witnessed there, not a single one alighted on a tree, most of them settling right on the ground in the alfalfa, while many got into the empty hives that were spread in windward direction for that purpose, notwithstanding the fact that swarming took place on very quiet, bright sunny days.

Something has probably to do with the fact that bees have a peculiar way of settling on the same spots where previous swarms have selected to alight. It is explained by bee-keepers that a swarm leaves a special odor at the place where it clustered, and other swarms are thereby attracted to the same place. Some Russian bee-keepers think the odor of the queen attracts the bees to the place where she once alighted.

It has also been observed that after-swarms frequently fly farther and settle on more elevated places than prime swarms. Young queens are more vigorous and not as heavy as their mother, therefore they can perform better flying feats than the former.

Now that the swarm has settled in a cluster, scouts are sent out to look for a new home. Whether the scouts depart before the swarm leaves the parent hive or shortly thereafter is rather difficult to determine. There were cases where emigrants left their hive and went home without ever stopping to cluster. More often, however, they clustered for a length of time, from fifteen minutes to perhaps a day or more, until they departed for a new home.

When they get to their new home, a number of the first comers stand on the alighting board and on the walls of the hive with abdomens lifted in the air and fan with their wings. This is probably their mode of notifying the bees left behind them of the new home they located. Soon they begin their steady, uninterrupted march homeward, if the queen is with them.

They settle to work presently without much loss of time. They form a curtain-like cluster and begin to build comb. There is not even a trace of that elemental, hilarious joy to which they had abandoned themselves completely just a short while ago. They are now very actively engaged in a thorough house cleaning of their new home, mature bees bring in pollen and nectar, and the queen begins to lay eggs as soon as the younger bees have built enough of comb to receive stores and eggs therein.

To return now to the so-called "parent colony." It may or may not cast off an after-swarm, much depending on the population of the bees left in the hive. Ordinarily the first young queen emerges from the cell in about eight days after the prime swarm left the hive. If no after-swarm is forthcoming, she may destroy her sisters in the remaining queen cells, the workers frequently tearing them open for that purpose. The virgin then runs restlessly around issuing some sharp notes, called by bee-keepers "piping," while her sisters in the cells answer her call, and are forthwith destroyed. She mates in about five or six days thereafter, and thus becomes the mother of a new colony.

California

Glossary

(A.=Arabic; H.=Hebrew; R.=Russian; Y.=Yiddish; *lit.*=literally)

Abele Zion (H.) — Mourners of Zion.

Aggadah, Aggadot (H.) — Legends and tales, especially those found in rabbinic literature.

Al-Isra (A.) — Mohammed's night journey from Mecca to Jerusalem.

Baḥurim (H., Y.) — Youths, i. e. students.

Bene Mikra' (H.) — *See* Karaites.

Bochur (=Baḥur, H., Y.), *see* Baḥurim.

Beth-Midrash (H., Y.) — House of study, synagogue.

Dorshei Da'at (H.) — Seekers of knowledge (Society in Philadelphia).

Farband (Y.)=Yiddisher Natzyonaler Arbeter Farband — Jewish Workers' Alliance of America. (Now, Labor Zionist Order).

Get (H.) — Bill of divorce.

Hadith (A.) — Collection of Mohammedan traditions.

Hajj (A.) — Pilgrimage.

Ḥaber (H.) — Member, title given to a scholar.

Ḥayye Neshamot (H.) — Soulful life.

Galuth (H.) — Exile, Diaspora. The Yiddish is *Golles*, any land outside of the Holy Land.

Islam (A.) — The religion of the Mohammedans.

Kad (H.) — Jug, pitcher.

Karaim (H.) — *see* Karaites.

Karaites (H.=Karaim) — A sect in Judaism founded and organized upon Sadducean principles by Anan b. David of Babylonia in the eighth century. The Karaites, also known as *Bene Mikra'* (Children, or Followers of the Scripture), observed only the commandments of the Torah and were opposed to Talmudic traditions and laws.

Ketubah (H.) — Marriage contract.

Khamr (A.) — Wine.

Kiddush (H.) — Blessing over wine (on Sabbaths and Festivals).

Korban Minḥah (H., Y.) — A Prayer-book with a translation in old-Yiddish mainly used by orthodox womenfolk.

Kopekes (R., Y.) — The Russian Rouble has 100 *Kopek*, i. e., pennies.

Koved (H., Y.) — Honor.

Kuzari — Name of a religious philosophical book by Judah Halevi.

Luftmenschen (Y.) — men without visible means of support, "men who lived on thin air."

Rikkub (H.) — Karaitic theory about married people being as one body.

Machen le-chayim (Y.) (*lit.*, make, or say "to (your) health") — Drink a toast.

Mashkeh (H., Y.) — Liquor, intoxicating beverage.

Mitzvah (H., Y.) (*lit.*, religious commandment) — good deed, benevolence.

Nabidh (A.) — An Arabian beverage made of honey.

Ru'ya (A.) — A vision.

Shema' (H.) (*lit.*, "Hear") — Jewish confession of faith, section of Deut. 6.4–8, recited in daily prayers.

Siḥat ḥullin (H.) — Idle talk, opposite of *Dibre Torah*, words of learning.

Shirei Ke'arah (H.) — Poems written on a plate and presented to newlyweds.

Shoḥet (H., Y.) — Ritual slaughterer.

Teḥines (Pl. of the sing. Teḥine = H. *Teḥinah*; H. Y.) — A special devotional, a Prayer-book of supplications and prayers in old-Yiddish, mainly used by orthodox womenfolk.

Tse'ena u-Re'enah (H., Y. — Tzene Rene) — A book of homiletical interpretations of the Five Books of Moses, composed by Rabbi Jacob Ashkenazi of Yanow (1550–1628) in old-Yiddish. First published in 1590, it became the most popular book among Jewish women all through the centuries. The title owes its name to the phrase Ze'ena u-re'ena (Go forth . . . and gaze . . .) in Cant. 3.11.

Yeshivah (H., Y. — pl. Yeshivot) — Rabbinical academy.

Yorzeit (Y.) (= Yahrtzeit) — Anniversary day of the death of a near relative.

Zedakah (H., Y.) (*lit.*, Righteousness) — charity.

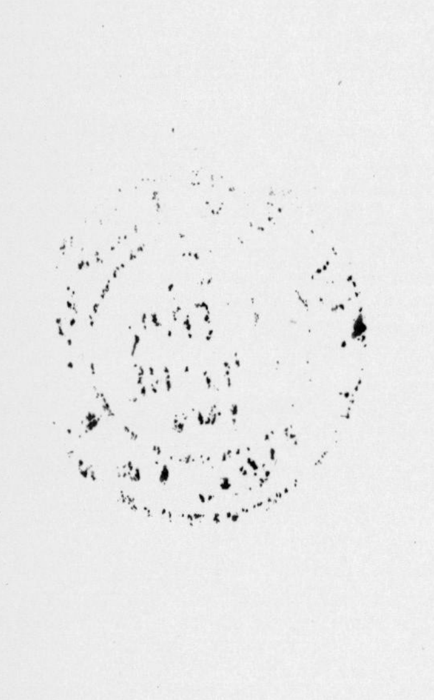